The Resurrection of Immortality

The Resurrection of Immortality

An Essay in Philosophical Eschatology

Mark S. McLeod-Harrison

CASCADE *Books* • Eugene, Oregon

THE RESURRECTION OF IMMORTALITY
An Essay in Philosophical Eschatology

Copyright © 2017 Mark S. McLeod-Harrison. All rights reserved. Except for brief quotations in critical publications or reviews, no part of this book may be reproduced in any manner without prior written permission from the publisher. Write: Permissions, Wipf and Stock Publishers, 199 W. 8th Ave., Suite 3, Eugene, OR 97401.

Cascade Books
An Imprint of Wipf and Stock Publishers
199 W. 8th Ave., Suite 3
Eugene, OR 97401

www.wipfandstock.com

PAPERBACK ISBN: 978-1-5326-1816-1
HARDCOVER ISBN: 978-1-4982-4349-0
EBOOK ISBN: 978-1-4982-4348-3

Cataloguing-in-Publication data:

Names: McLeod-Harrison, Mark S., 1956–

Title: The resurrection of immortality : an essay in philosophical eschatology / Mark McLeod-Harrison.

Description: Eugene, OR: Cascade Books, 2017 | Includes bibliographical references and index.

Identifiers: ISBN 978-1-5326-1816-1 (paperback) | ISBN 978-1-4982-4349-0 (hardcover) | ISBN 978-1-4982-4348-3 (ebook)

Subjects: LCSH: Soul | Mind and body | Theological anthropology | Future life | Immortality | Philosophical theology | Christianity—Philosophy

Classification: BD423 M427 2017 (print) | BD423 (ebook)

Manufactured in the U.S.A. JULY 21, 2017

In memory of Robert N. Wennberg,
and in honor of Stanley R. Obitts,
my undergraduate philosophy teachers.

Contents

Preface ... ix
Acknowledgements ... xiii

1. Varieties of Mortality ... 1
2. Varieties of Immortality ... 20
3. Can God Cause Humans to Cease to Exist? ... 28
4. Why Humans Can't Bring about Their Soul-Death ... 44
5. An Argument for Immutable Immortality ... 51

Appendix A: Some Speculative Metaphysical Structure ... 71
Appendix B: Is Annihilation Worse Than Everlasting Torment? ... 80
Appendix C: Soul Euthanasia and the Emptying of Hell ... 90

Bibliography ... 103
Index ... 105

Preface

Immortal, invisible, God only wise

—Walter C. Smith, 1876

When I was a teenager, a popular Christian evangelism tract had the question "If you died tonight, do you know where you'd be going?" emblazoned across its 2-inch-by-4-inch cover. One obvious response to that question, then as now, is "to the mortuary." But what if, many people wonder, there is a life after death? In traditional Christian thought and practice, belief in the afterlife has often been writ large. What is the nature of heaven, hell, and purgatory? Who goes where, when, under what conditions? Will we have bodies? Is there soul sleep between physical death and resurrection? These and many other questions have been, and are, debated among Christians. Behind all these questions, however, is a more logically fundamental issue, viz., immortality.

Having a life after death does not guarantee immortality. Within the Christian faith, however, it is common to think that if one survives beyond one's physical death, then one goes on existing forever, either with God in heaven or without God in hell. To engage with Christian eschatology about the afterlife would require both theological and (biblical) exegetical skills that go beyond mine. I write neither as a theologian nor as a biblical exegete. I write as a philosopher. But I do write as a Christian and, as such, I make certain assumptions about the Christian faith, including that there is an afterlife. Granted that there is an afterlife, we might wonder what philosophical grounds can be provided for it.

Lots of people, from Plato to MacTaggart, have provided arguments for immortality. I wish to contribute to that long line of thought. So I provide here my version of an argument for immortality. But it will be helpful to know my motivation for doing so.

Eschatology has not been a central focus of my philosophical thought. Indeed, when my (largely) Christian students ask me my views, my answer is short and direct. "Jesus is coming back" and "I hope someday to be fully in the presence of God." That's it. Nothing too detailed there. But maybe it's my age (not dead yet, but my father died at sixty-three and I turn sixty-one next week). Or maybe it was some comment I read by Richard Rorty that implied that heaven would be an uninteresting place because we'd have all the answers. Or maybe it was some other experience I had. But in the fall of 2015 I offered an undergraduate class on heaven and hell and I uncovered lots of serious debate about annihilationism that I'd not encountered before. I'd long thought that annihilationism—the view that at judgment or some finite time after it the unredeemed (should there be any) will cease to exist—was a superior position over notions of hell implying eternal, conscious torment (or "ECT"). Although the latter has been the overwhelmingly common view on the afterlife for the unredeemed, I found, and still find, the doctrine pernicious.

Annihilationism is founded on what's called "conditional immortality." If humans are created by God as immortal, then at our physical deaths we must either be present with God forever or outside God's presence in hell, for not even God can cause an immortal being to cease to be. In order for God to cause or allow our annihilation, humans would have to begin our existence as mortals and be granted (if redeemed) immortality at a later point. Immortality is thus conditional on our redemption. When I began to think about conditional immortality I discovered what I thought were good reasons to think that humans are not, in fact, created mortal but that we are immortal from our natality. By pursuing this line of thought, however, I undermined my own belief in annihilationism. Immortality had been, from my point of view, at least, resurrected and annihilation annihilated. And so this short book was born.

The glorious Victorian hymn I quote above makes clear that the writer thought only God was wise. But is God also the only immortal one as well? In some sense, yes. Only God is *independently* immortal, for the immortality of God depends on no one other than the divine self. Human immortality, it seems to me, is of a different order. Why? Before I could answer that, I felt a prior question needed a response. That first question is this: If we are immortal in something like the traditional Christian sense of immortality,

Preface

what reasons are there to think so, independent of the testimony of the Christian Scriptures? Given a commonly held set of beliefs about the Christian God, I think that there is an argument for the case that not even God can cause humans to cease to exist. Arguments for immortality often suggest that God, because of love, will not annihilate anyone. I don't believe such moral arguments are strong enough to ground a metaphysically significant account of immortality. The argument provided is a metaphysical rather than a moral argument and hence provides a better reason to think that humans are, once created, immortal and cannot be annihilated.

That returned me to the nature of human immortality, and so my second question is this: What is the metaphysical structure that undergirds human immortality? I provide what I hope is a careful analysis of the concepts of mortality and immortality along with a tentative, but plausible, account of the metaphysics of relevant properties. Many contemporary philosophers think of properties as necessities. That is, like propositions, numbers, and other abstract entities, properties exist temporally forever (or they exist atemporally) as well as non-spatially and in a causally inert manner. As such, they are thought to be necessarily existent. I propose an alternative to that notion based on the work of Tom Morris. Instead of immortality being an essential property of humans, I propose that it is an immutable property. This somewhat chastened view of properties allows for immortality to be a property true of humans, but not a property we had to have to be human per se.

My intention in writing is not, ultimately, to convince anyone outside the Christian faith that humans are, in fact, immortal. Rather, it is entirely an "in-house" project written primarily for Christian theologians and philosophers. But it is a work in philosophy rather than scriptural exegesis or theological eschatology. It is, given broadly Christian assumptions about God, an exercise in philosophical eschatology.

Chapter 1 attempts to give a conceptual account of mortality and identifies various ways one might succumb to mortality. Chapter 2 describes immortality along with a conceptual map of kinds of immortality. Chapter 3 analyzes one sort of argument for the conclusion that humans are mortal in the sense that God can bring about the end of human existence. That argument is found wanting. Chapter 4 argues for the claim that humans cannot bring about their own soulish end. Chapter 5 argues that immortality is an immutable property, a property such that once one has it one cannot lose it and there never was a time in one's existence when one didn't have it. Immutable properties are distinct from essential properties in that all essential properties are immutable properties but not all immutable properties are essential. There are three appendices. Appendix A is a brief exploration of some metaphysical claims that could be true, and that if true would allow for a larger philosophical framework for the claims of the argument for immortality. The second appendix considers whether eternal conscious punishment is worse than annihilation. The final appendix presents an argument that points toward, but is not conclusive evidence for, a universalist account of human salvation, thus ameliorating the propensity of some to use the immortality of humans as springboard to defending hell as a place of eternal, conscious punishment.

Acknowledgements

My thanks to Phil Smith for reading the manuscript and its ancestors. Michael Almeida also kept me from various modal misunderstandings and pointed me in the direction of Tom Morris's essay covering stable properties. I want to thank Robin Parry for his as ever excellent editorial advice on this book. Thanks to Paula Hampton, the administrative assistant for the College of Christian Studies at George Fox University, for her copyediting and for preparing my manuscript for publication. I also thank the students in my Fall 2015 class on heaven and hell for their lively discussion of the issues surrounding Christian eschatology. Any mistakes in reasoning or presentation are mine.

C. S. Lewis wrote:

> There are no ordinary people. You have never talked to a mere mortal. Nations, cultures, arts, civilizations—these are mortal, and their life is to ours as the life of a gnat. But it is immortals whom we joke with, work with, marry, snub and exploit—immortal horrors or everlasting splendors. This does not mean that we are to be perpetually solemn. We must play. But our merriment must be of that kind (and it is, in fact, the merriest kind) which exists between people who have, from the outset, taken each other seriously—no flippancy, no superiority, no presumption.[1]

I first read those lines when I taught at Westmont College with many excellent colleagues. Two of those colleagues were Robert Wennberg and Stan Obitts.

Bob was one of my undergraduate teachers in philosophy at Westmont College and later my friend and colleague. He was a wonderful teacher, an excellent philosopher, and one of the wisest people I have ever known. If the thesis of this book is true, then Bob is still around, perhaps doing more philosophy, but at the very least, living more fully in love than the

1. Lewis, *The Weight of Glory*, 46.

immortals left here on earth. While I thanked Bob while he was incarnate here with us, I want to honor Bob for being the good friend and mentor he was to me when I was a student and a much younger "professional" philosopher. He truly knew how to treat others as the immortals they are and I thank him for the wisdom and love he showed to others.

Stan is another immortal who was also one of my undergraduate philosophy teachers. He too became a colleague and friend. Stan was a meticulous reader of texts and he had a way, as my mother would say, "of putting the fear of God into you." Stan's teaching was rigorous and thorough. My recollection is of Stan sitting at the head of the seminar table, going around to each student asking in turn what some sentence or other from the day's reading meant. One had to be on one's intellectual toes. Stan was and remains passionate about Christian apologetics and he believes deeply in the value of the liberal arts for all Christian students. I learned much from him even though I suspect he and I disagree about a good many things in philosophy. Stan is long retired from Westmont, but his influence is very much alive in his many students who went on for doctoral work in philosophy. I want to thank him for his many years of service to evangelical Christian higher education.

This book is dedicated to Stan, and in memory of Bob—friends and colleagues both.

CHAPTER 1

Varieties of Mortality

Although this chapter is fundamentally about the nature of mortality, it has the aim of setting the stage for the next chapter dealing with immortality. I want to situate the entire conversation among the plethora of possible ways of thinking about the topic first before moving on to immortality and mortality proper. This will help us identify focused understandings of immortality and mortality before those notions are analyzed. In this chapter, I then turn to mortality, picking up immortality in chapter 2.

I

Some contemporary theorists suggest that we might develop biological immortality, by which they mean that while we won't avoid death, we can stop aging.[1] Others propose that with nanotechnology, we might keep ourselves alive for a lot longer than what can be achieved by not aging. We might even "record" ourselves, some suggest, into sophisticated computers. Thus we might "reconstruct" ourselves by technology so as to, in effect, live on forever, at least in principle.[2] On such notions, one might exist forever in one's own (modified) body, or embodied in another form (a computerized body). Of course, the "body" in question would need a great number of improvements over our current ones.

While these may count as immortalities in a loose sense of the term, they are not my concern here. Nor are the sorts of immortalities that one

---

1. Despain, "How to Achieve 'Biological Immortality' Naturally."
2. Guadin, "Nanotech Could Make Humans Immortal by 2040, Futurist Says."

can find in some Eastern religious or philosophical accounts, where the self is understood to merge or simply be identical with ultimate reality. In Advaita Vedanta Hinduism, for example, atman is Brahman.[3] When our time on the wheel of karma is complete, we come to know the truth that our individuality is something of an illusion.[4] This sort of immortality is not personal, for in some sense the individual self is engulfed in some greater whole. Neither is it personal immortality to understand "immortality" to be a sort of ongoing cultural or familiar influence a person might have on those surviving the person's death. Finally, one might say that humans are immortal in the recycling of food-stuff from one's deceased body into compost. That's not personal immortality either.

These "immortalities" are, of course, different from one another and hence can be taken as varieties of immortality, but they are not the sort of variety I take up. I want to focus on more traditional Western notions (although the West has no private ownership of the idea) where one personally exists forever (without the aids of mechanical or human biological interference). The immortality I will focus on is picked out, in a very general way, by the notion of human persons existing forever as the persons we are from our creation as individuals. I'll call this "personal immortality."[5]

Within personal immortality, one can find two other sorts of variety. The first varietal grouping has three members: the continuation of the soul separate from the body, the resurrection of the person in a body continuous with the earthy one (in whatever sense is necessary for identifying the latter body with the former), and continuation of the person in the person's "real" body (typically thought of as a sort of astral or second body).[6] Once again, these varieties of immortality are not my main concern here. I won't,

---

3. "Atman" is, roughly, the individual human soul, whereas "Brahman" refers to ultimate reality, sometimes understood as the "world soul." So my soul is the world soul.

4. This is a very truncated version of *advaita vedanta* Hinduism. Of course there are many other versions of the afterlife in Hinduism and versions of Buddhism as well. I won't comment further on them.

5. The notions of personal immortality and having one's present biological life extended forever could be combined. The Christian doctrine of resurrection suggests that my body must first biologically die, however. Nevertheless, there is nothing, so far as I can see, incoherent with the idea that instead of passing through biological death one simply has one's body reconstituted so as to achieve immortality without biological death. We may see cases of this with the biblical Enoch and Elijah (and in Catholic tradition, Mary)—none of whom passed through physical death, but instead were assumed into the presence of God. Having recognized this possibility, I will not pick it up again.

6. See Edwards, *Introduction to Immortality*, 4–5.

in other words, explore these options at any length or attempt to decide which of these (or other possibilities) might be the case. I want to consider, instead, the varieties of personal immortality simpliciter. Personal immortality simpliciter opens the door to a second sort of variety. What varieties of immortality might there be for the individual person regardless of what sort of vehicle one obtains immortality in—a disembodied soul, a resurrected body, or an astral body? If humans are, or can be, immortal, what sorts of immortality might be available for those having it? Are there, in fact, different sorts of immortality for those who have it?

II

As I've noted, my main concern is immortality, but a good way to understand immortality and its varieties is through mortality and its varieties. Thus, the remainder of this chapter is given over to thinking about mortality. This section is dedicated to considering connections between death and mortality. Section III takes up two questions. First, under what conditions might one be thought to be have succumbed to mortality?[7] Second, are there different kinds of mortality corresponding to those conditions? I suggest a variety of conditions under which one might be thought to have succumbed to mortality, and I think the answer to the latter question is affirmative.

One can hardly grasp immortality without considering mortality. Immortality is a negative concept, something like the concept *infinite*. And like the concept of infinity—where we have a fairly clear notion of the finite, whereas the infinite is more complicated—so we have a fairly clear notion of the mortal, whereas immortality is more complicated. That is not to say that finitude or mortality are easily grasped notions. Perhaps because we have a great deal of experience with death—that is, the death of others—we may think mortality is easily described. Indeed, it seems that we have a good handle on mortality, one that is captured in an aphorism: "all humans are mortal." That is, we all die. When a person dies, she ceases to be—her mortality, so to speak, catches up to her. Thus, *death* and *mortal* are closely related terms; sometimes they are even taken as virtual synonyms. To be mortal simply means, in some contexts, to be one who dies. Indeed, the

---

7. In English, the term *mortal* is both a noun (She is a mortal) and an adjective (She is mortal), but it has no verb form, unlike the term *death*. One can die, but one cannot "mort" or "mortalize." So I use the phrase, "succumb to mortality" as a near substitute.

term "mortal" comes from the Latin *mors/mort-*, which means "death." But caution is called for here.

As a first attempt at understanding the term *mortality*, we might say that to be mortal is to be the sort of thing that at some point in time ceases to exist. This implies a couple of things. First, to cease to exist one must already exist and one must move from being existent to being non-existent. Second, and related to the first, things that once existed but no longer exist are, arguably, no longer mortal. Once having ceased to exist, one can no longer be said to be mortal. To say "one is mortal" requires existence. But existence ought not be confused with being. (See the discussion below where I introduce the work of Yourgrau.) Third, although we can say a non-existent thing was mortal, not every non-existent thing was mortal. Some non-existent things never had existence to lose—for example, humans not yet conceived. Fourth, lots of things are mortal, not just living things. We could speak of, say rocks, as mortal. They exist and can come to not exist. However, we typically apply the term *mortal* only to living things—humans and other animals, at least, but plants as well. We speak of all these things, at least, as dying. We tend not to speak of rocks as dying and in accord with that, it's not clear that rocks are mortal. Usual English usage aside, if mortality deals only with existent things becoming non-existent, there's no clear reason to think non-living things are not mortal as well. On those grounds, and to shift the ground momentarily to immortality, abstract objects might be said to be immortal. Plato's forms were "immortal" and on the basis that human souls are like the forms, they too were thought immortal. God, as well, who can be said to be alive, but not, strictly speaking, alive in the biological sense, is thought to be immortal. Mortality and immortality trade in existence and non-existence, not life and death, at least fundamentally.

Of course, we can restrict our usage of the term and in doing so limit the scope of the terms *mortal* and *immortal* to living things. Under such a restriction, presumably, living things will need to continue living in order to be immortal. We can talk, then, of things being mortal or immortal in terms of whether they continue to live, because presumably continuing to live is a necessary component of continuing to exist. However, I will use the term *live* broadly so that it is not merely biological entities (animals and plants) that are alive, but God, angels, and possibly other sorts of beings as well. God is alive (should the divinity exist), even if not biologically so, as are angels and demons alive (if such there be). My focus, however, is on humans and their mortality (or immortality) and I won't concern myself with God, angels, demons, or for that matter non-human animals or plants. I'll have enough on my philosophical plate merely taking on the notions of human mortality or immortality. If there is an exception to this self-limited context, I'll note it.

To further narrow my concern, I'll think of being alive as involving something like personhood. Broadly speaking, because God, angels, and demons can be said to be personal (if they exist), they can be said to be alive. It would follow that some non-human animals—at least those furthest removed from humans—are not alive in the relevant sense. I think we would be hard pressed to say that amoebas can be well described as personal. Whether or not they are personal is not something I need to explore. Chimps, elephants, dolphins, and other animals are almost certainly personal, even if not as richly personal as humans. Further, there may be all sorts of things in the universe that are personal of which we know nothing. But it's certainly not clear where the dividing line between personal and impersonal life should be drawn and I will not attempt to draw it. Again, my focus is *human* immortality. So henceforth, when I speak of mortality and immortality, I'll be working in the context of the personal living entities we are ourselves: humans.

Thus, mortality is closely connected to the loss of one's personal life, rather than the "mere" loss of existence. It is no accident, then, that many contemporary philosophers take physical death just to be non-existence. As such, death and mortality are linked by association. While I have no interest in claiming that death (at least the physical death of personal beings) and mortality are identical (they certainly need not be), one can learn a good deal about mortality by making that assumption, albeit temporarily.

It is helpful to note that the term *death* is ambiguous. Stephen Rosenbaum suggests that it's useful "to distinguish three concepts from one another, those of dying, death, and being dead."[8] Dying is the process by which one becomes dead; being dead is the state one is in, so to speak, after one dies; and death is the (metaphorical) portal one passes through in moving from dying to being dead. The "portal" here could merely be a temporal marker, the instant at which living ends and being dead begins. To summarize, "death comes at the end of a person's dying, and at the beginning of a person's being dead."[9] Now if we assume that death just is non-existence, we would have the following distinctions: Becoming non-existent, quitting

---

8. Rosenbaum, "How to be Dead," 120.
9. Ibid., 121.

existence, and being non-existent. The middle phrase—quitting existence—isn't a happy one, but one can only press the language so far. It is meant to capture the "portal" that comes at the end of becoming non-existent and the beginning of being non-existent.

Palle Yourgrau suggests the following account of death: "By 'death' I will mean precisely: 'permanent postnatal nonexistence.' By this definition, however, I do not mean to settle either the linguistic issue of what the English word 'really means' or the factual question of whether, in this sense, anyone ever really dies."[10] I want to make some brief comments about Yourgrau's definition. First, by "death" presumably Yourgrau intends what Rosenbaum calls "being dead." Second, Yourgrau leaves open the possibility that there are senses of the English term *death* that do not, themselves, entail non-existence. Nevertheless, for his purposes, he ignores them. In short, what he really wants to talk about is the post-natal, permanent, non-existence of the human person, and he simply identifies that with physical death. It could, in fact, be identified with other things—perhaps the death of the immaterial soul, for example. Something that could occur at some time well past physical death.

Using Rosenbaum's distinctions and Yourgrau's definition, it's important to note the concepts of death and mortality do not map neatly onto each other, if at all. One can say "she is dead," but that is not the same as saying "she is mortal." Although in daily English usage we might use the term *mortal* as a stand-in for *death* (consider the actuary's "mortality tables," which could just as well be called "death tables"), typically "mortality" is not substitutable for "death." Being dead implies that one was mortal, but being mortal does not imply that one is dead. One is mortal, presumably, before one is dead. Indeed, one might say that one cannot be both dead and mortal. If the dead do not exist, then to say a dead person—say Socrates—is mortal is to say that a non-existent person can cease to exist and that claim is at least slightly paradoxical. Strictly speaking, a dead person is not mortal. Mortality, in an odd twist of the English language, is future oriented. Thus, to be mortal is to be the sort of thing that will cease to exist at some point in time not yet reached.

But perhaps that isn't right. Yourgrau also asks the following: "How can one even assert, for example, that Socrates is dead? If this is a truth, whom is it supposed to be a truth about? Socrates? But there is, there exists, no such person. For, precisely because he is dead, he is no longer, and therefore

---

10. Yourgrau, "The Dead," 139.

there is no one of whom we may truly predicate death, or nonexistence."[11] On Yourgrau's account, one can understand death via the claim that "death concerns the nonexistent as well as the existent; that, therefore, some things do not exist—i.e., that there are nonexistent objects. We should distinguish, therefore, between being something, being an object . . . and [in contrast] being an existing object."[12] So for Yourgrau, even though a person is dead and hence nonexistent, one can still refer to the object that that person is and attribute nonexistence to that person. In short, on Yourgrau's position, being an object does not entail that the object exists. Whether an object exists is a further question beyond whether the object is. The dead are objects who once existed but who no longer do. Their "permanent" objecthood does not grant them permanent existence. They are not, in other words, immortal simply for being objects. To be immortal would require not merely that one is an object but also that one is an *existing* object who will never fail to exist (once having come into existence). For all that, however, the term *mortal* does not apply to those who are dead, for the dead do not exist and mortality calls attention to the fact that a mortal who exists will—at some point in time—cease to exist. So not only do the dead tell no lies, they're not mortal either.

If we bring these observations over from Yourgrau's talk of death to mortality, one whose mortality has come to fruition is one who once existed but does so no more. Such a person is an object without existence. But being an object—even when an object is taken as always having being (but not necessarily existence)—does not imply immortality though the object always is (that is, has being but not existence).

But here we run into problems. It is only the existent that can become non-existent. To say of someone that she is dead is to say that she is nonexistent. So while we can say "some humans are dead" and thereby intend "some humans are (postnatally) non-existent" we can hardly say "some humans with objecthood but who do not exist are humans who cease to exist." Although the concept of mortality clearly deals in death and non-existence, it is not simply death or non-existence. So when we say someone is mortal, we mean that she will, at some point in the future, become non-existent.

---

11. Ibid., 138.

12. Ibid., 142. This point can be made in logical symbolism that keeps the ideas straight. If we use ($\exists x$) to stand for "there is" and "E!" as a predicate "exits" then we can say "there are objects that don't exist" this way: ($\exists x$)~E!x. Although generally I'll keep the logical symbolism to a minimum in this essay, sometimes it is helpful to have more precision at hand than ordinary language allows.

So the claim "all humans are mortal" must be taken to mean "All existing humans are mortal." Dead humans, although still humans in the "object" sense, are not existing.

So a mortal is someone who is both existent and who will, at some point in the future, become non-existent. When we speak of mortality, however, we don't simply have in mind what Rosenbaum calls "death"—the portal through which one passes. We often have in mind that our deaths are proximate, that is, immanently present or close to hand. Our lives can end, in other words, at any time. So although somewhat misleading, we might say that a mortal is becoming non-existent. This latter is close to Rosenbaum's notion of dying, but we need to modify it somewhat. Usually when we say someone is dying we mean to say that her death is near or perhaps that she has an illness that will bring about the state of death even if it is not near. This seems to be what Rosenbaum has in mind. One might discover that one has late-stage cancer and there is nothing medically to be done—one has only a couple of months to live. One is thus dying. Or perhaps one discovers that one has a fatal sort of cancer, but it is slow moving. Perhaps one will live for five or six years. The clearer use of "dying" is the former, but one can use it in the latter case as well. There is much ambiguity with the notion of dying. The person with slow-moving but fatal cancer can fight it. Hence, he might say "I'm not dying yet" even though he might believe on some level that he is. However, the term "dying" is more elastic than even these claims indicate.

Before pursuing that elasticity further, note that there are also cases where a person dies but we would not say of him that he is dying. Someone killed "instantaneously" in an auto accident would not say "I'm not dying yet" as he drives down the highway and we would not use the term "dying" of him even a second or two before the accident. We would have no access to such information. In some sense, he doesn't go through a "dying" stage. Rather, he just passes through the death portal. Whether one uses the phrase "is dying" depends a lot on the circumstance. Once again, the term "dying" is more elastic than we might think.

It is so elastic that one might say—with plausibility—that one is dying from the moment one has natality. (By "natality" I simply mean the beginning of life.)[13] Although sometimes we say jokingly, that one begins

---

13. There are some important issues here. The non-existent but pre-natality human—humans who could exist but do not yet—pose some interesting questions. Why do we fear non-existence as it emerges in death but not non-existence of our "beings" prior to life? Again, by "natality" I simply mean the beginning of (personal) life, whenever that

to die the moment one is born, philosophers from Plato to Heidegger have suggested that humans are "beings toward death." The point is that in some sense mortality emerges with natality. Now this sort of understanding is not, presumably, what Rosenbaum has in mind when he speaks of one's dying. But it does draw together the notion of dying with the notion of mortality, and our mortality is always at hand even if, strictly speaking, our actual death may be some time off. One can die anytime, once begun. So although we don't usually say things like "her mortality is close at hand" we could, and I suppose that by saying so, one might be calling attention to her dying—the process in Rosenbaum's sense. Dying just is succumbing to mortality. But just as one might say we are dying from the moment we are born, so one could say we are mortal. Once born, we are going to die and, in fact, we can die anytime.

Having learned what we can from thinking about (physical) death as mortality, I want to turn to a more neutral position. I'll use the term *soul* to pick out the aspect (or aspects) of the human person the cessation of which brings to an end forever the existence of the individual human being. "Soul," that is, picks out the essential features of the human person where losing (any one of or all) those features entails the non-existence of the person. It is at the death of the soul that one's mortality comes home to roost. Notice, however, that "soul" is neutral among dualism and materialism and the host of views represented by those terms. If one adopts a materialist understanding of the human person such that existence as a human person depends essentially on a functioning human body, then when one dies, one ceases to exist, but only if there is no resurrection (or other plausible alternative) in the offing. If one adopts a dualist perspective, then one may exist beyond one's bodily death. It does not follow from that, however, that one is not mortal for one's (dualistic) soul might become non-existent at some point. It is the death of the essence of the human person that I am concerned to discuss, whatever it happens to be.

We are thus free to speak of the death of the soul and thus identify the death of the soul with permanent, post-natal, non-existence. One does not thereby beg any questions about when that occurs or whether it is tied to the functioning human body or something else. On such a view, it is with the death of the soul that mortality enters the play. To avoid confusion, I will use the term *death* as we usually do, viz., to pick out that point at which a human person moves from being physically alive to being physically dead,

is for humans.

and the term *soul-death* to refer to that point at which a human person moves from being existent to non-existent. In other words, "soul-death" is equivalent to "permanent, post-natal, non-existence of the human person." Thus, it is possible that one can die without attaining soul-death, but it is equally possible that one attains soul-death by dying. Whether one can in fact attain soul-death by dying turns on whether the body's continuing to live (perhaps in resurrected form) is an essential property of being human. Note too that one can continue with a parallel to Rosenbaum's tripartite division of dying, death, and being dead by speaking of soul-dying, soul-death, and being soul-dead.

If one is soul-dead, one is no longer mortal and correspondingly, if one soul-dies then one was mortal but no longer is mortal, for one no longer exists. As noted above, being mortal implies that one is alive—in our case, soul-alive. As pointed out above, mortality is, oddly enough, oriented toward the future. The soul-dead have no future, of course. The unconceived are not (yet) mortal and may never be. Living things, so far as we typically experience them, are temporal beings. So since it is living beings who are mortal, and since non-living beings cannot cease to be soul-alive, mortality is future-oriented.

What of when we say things such as "all humans are mortal?" We mean to include past and future humans as well. But to say "all humans are mortal" is just to say that "all humans that are, have been, or will be existent are, have been, or will be mortal." Mortality is true only of the existent so long as they exist, and all existents, in our general experience, are temporal. Any soul-death that occurs to them occurs while they exist through time. Once they are soul-dead, time, arguably, affects them no more.

Now if God is alive, and if God's life is atemporal, it seems that God's immortality is not a matter of living forever but rather living without time. So immortality may not be future-oriented in the same way mortality is. For humans, soul-dying, or at the very least soul-death, occurs at a time. One changes from one time to another from being existent to non-existent. Such a change simply can't occur atemporally. Mortality implies a change, immortality need not. Only temporal beings can be mortal and so long as they exist, they exist temporally. To say that such a person is mortal is to say that while existent, the person is mortal. Thus, to say "all humans are mortal" is to say "all *existent* humans are mortal," which is to say "all existent humans become non-existent humans." So it is difficult to shed references to time from discussions of mortality. All existent humans, during their existence, will enter soul-death and exist no more. I will assume these points in what follows.

I want to understand the statement "All humans are mortal." But to understand that statement, we need to grasp mortality. If mortality deals only in soul-death, then to say "All humans are mortal" is to say "All humans soul-die." But there are several ways of understanding the connection between mortality and soul-death. Here are three ways.

1. To be mortal is to be such that *possibly* one soul-dies.
2. To be mortal is to be such that one soul-dies.
3. To be mortal is to be such that *necessarily* one soul-dies.

These three ways of understanding mortality are nested. If one necessarily soul-dies then one soul-dies and if one soul-dies then one possibly soul-dies. But of course, the reverse is not the case. The possibility of one's soul-dying does not suggest either that one does soul-die or that one necessarily soul-dies. Having said that, we need to look closer at each of 1–3. Since there are different senses of "possibility" and "necessity," it will be important to identify what sense of each I'm using.

To consider 1, we need to distinguish between a logical and an epistemic sense of "possibility." In saying possibly one soul-dies we might be saying that, *for all we know*, humans soul-die or they do not. Although we can't ignore the epistemic version completely, it is not the main focus here, for I'm interested in the metaphysics of the mortality. So I take it that 1 makes the claim that it is broadly logically possible that mortals soul-die. Whenever there are modal terms about (terms dealing with possibility and necessity, "can" and "must"), it is wise to note the difference between what philosophers call *de dicto* and *de re* senses of modality. *De dicto* modal claims deal with the statements, whereas *de re* statements deal with things. So there is a difference between saying "Possibly, all mortals soul-die" and "All mortals possibly soul-die." It is helpful to capture this difference in logical symbolism. So where "M" stands for "is mortal" and "S" stands for "soul-dies," and "◊" is read "it is logically possible that"

1a. $\Diamond(x)(Mx \rightarrow Sx)$ It is logically possible that if one is mortal then one soul-dies.

1b. $(x)(Mx \rightarrow \Diamond Sx)$ If one is mortal then logically possibly one soul-dies.

The first gives a *de dicto* reading, the second a *de re* reading. The *de dicto* reading merely suggests that it could be the case that being mortal is sufficient for soul-death. It is equally true that it is possible that mortality is not sufficient for soul-death. That is not what I mean by 1.

Instead, I intend 1b, the *de re* reading. The *de re* reading suggests that each thing that is mortal possibly soul-dies. Being mortal, in other words, does not entail that one does as a matter of fact soul-die, only that one is the sort of thing that *can* soul-die. On the *de re* reading, 1 does not suggest either that the mortal thing must soul-die or even that it does, as a matter of fact, soul-die. In philosopher's jargon, in some possible worlds a given mortal soul-dies but in other possible worlds, the very same (trans-worldly) identical mortal does not soul-die. What this comes to, for our purposes here, is that soul-death is a contingent property of mortals. All mortality comes to is the possibility that one ceases to be and that claim is consistent with the factual state of affairs that one continues to exist forever. The possibility of one's soul-death is not sufficient for one's actual soul-death.

One might wonder, on those terms, whether in some possible worlds the individual is immortal in the sense that the person, in that world, never, as a matter of fact, soul-dies. Of course, the person, being mortal, could soul-die at any moment. Suppose, for example, we are able at some point to genetically engineer ourselves so that we not only don't age, but don't ever get ill. A person under this sort of scientific magic will, all other things being equal, live on and on. She is still mortal, however, for she could still cease to be—say by an accident. Even if she lives on forever, she would always be mortal in the sense captured by 1b. The person's continuing to exist, on these terms, would be entirely (logically) accidental, just as would the person's ceasing to exist. She would not, in other words, be essentially immortal. This appears to be the sort of immortality that attaches to the Greek gods who apparently are immortal so long as they consume nectar and ambrosia. Or they are immortal in the sense that they cannot die by natural means (given their internal structure, they will never die) but can, in some instances, be killed (by an outside force).

Although one might mean by "mortal" that it is possible that one soul-dies, typically it seems that we mean something stronger. We do not merely mean by "all humans are mortal" that one could cease to be, but might not. As noted, if we limit ourselves for a moment to speak of physical death, there is in some sense in which we could be mortal in the way 1 proposes. Those who think that humans may be capable of biological immortality have in mind just this sort of potential immortality. All the while, however, the so-called "biological immortals" will be capable of dying—they just won't die of their own accord, there being no "natural" breakdown of cellular life. Nevertheless, the "biological immortal" will remain mortal in the sense I've been working with here. One's death would come about through external means and not by "natural," internal means. If we broaden the account to consider soul-death, the same logic applies. A sort of functional immorality might be possible, but the functional immortal will remain mortal in the sense identified in the last few paragraphs. I will say that those who escape soul-death accidentally are *functionally* immortal, not truly immortal. Functional immortality would be a dicey proposition, able to end at any point.

The second suggestion, 2, also has two interpretations. One way to think about it is to ask how it is true, viz., is it accidentally true or nomologically true. As a first attempt at understanding 2 we might suggest

2a. Mortals accidentally but universally soul-die.

However, unless there is something inherent in the individuals who soul-die that explains why they all soul-die, the universality is puzzling. As such, whether 2a is true would involve a "wait-and-see" situation for, say, a temporal but omniscient onlooker. Since soul-death is accidental, whether mortals universally soul-die would remain an open proposition so long as mortals continue to exist. To get something stronger, one needs some reason to explain 2a's dual attribution of accidental universality.

Having an accidental property does not, of course, mean there is no explanation for why a thing has the property. There is, presumably, a nomological reason (or set of reasons) why some humans have hair, for example, and others do not. If an accidental property attends a certain kind of thing universally, then there is a nomological reason why it does. But then perhaps it is better to interpret 2 as

2b. It is nomologically necessary that mortals soul-die.

That something has a certain property nomologically (i.e., because of conditions falling under a law) explains why the property is present universally without the property being necessary to the thing. Natural laws (according to the vast majority of philosophers) are contingent, not logically necessary. Nevertheless, when in place they bring about their results universally upon the appropriate conditions being met. It does not follow from this universality, however, that events generated out of conditions and the attending laws are logically necessary.

Does natural nomological necessity apply to mortality as we are considering it? If soul-death were merely the death of the physical body, one might be tempted to stop the discussion here. Given the nature of the human body and the laws of biology, chemistry, and physics, then humans die because eventually the body comes into conditions that fulfill the demands of the physical laws. But if there is more to the soul than the biological life of the body, it is less clear what natural laws would bring about a mortal's soul-demise. So unless death is equivalent to soul-death, we'll need something more than natural laws to explain the universal nature of mortality.

What of some stronger sense of necessity? Here we turn to 3.

3. To be mortal is to be such that necessarily one soul-dies.

Again, when modal terms are introduced, one must take care to distinguish *de dicto* and *de re* understandings. Again, we might understand 3 as "Necessarily, all mortals soul-die" or "All mortals necessarily soul-die." In logical symbolism, where "□" is read "It is necessary that" and "M" is understood as "is mortal" and "S" is understood as "soul-dies" then 3 might be understood *de dicto*

3a. □(x)(Mx→Sx) Necessarily, if x is mortal, x soul-dies.

or *de re*

3b. (x)(Mx→□Sx) If x is mortal, necessarily x soul-dies.

The *de dicto* reading could be true while the *de re* reading false.

In fact, the *de re* reading seems far too strong. Think of this. "All bachelors are necessarily unmarried" is false (the state of marriage is accidental to one's person—bachelors could become married) but "necessarily all bachelors are unmarried" is true (it's definitional that a bachelor is unmarried—but there need not be any bachelors). Just like that, "all mortals necessarily soul-die" could be false even though "necessarily all mortals soul-die" could be true. *De re* readings of necessity are typically understood by philosophers to attribute essential characteristics to the subject. That is to say, if something has an essential property, in whatever possible world the subject exists, it has that property.

To attribute this sort of logical essentialism in regard to mortality to, say, humans, is too strong. Surely God could make humans immortal. In other words, surely there are possible worlds in which humans are not mortal. Nevertheless, it could be true that necessarily it is the case that all mortals soul-die. What's up for grabs is whether, in fact, anyone is actually mortal.

But what of a sense of necessity weaker than logical necessity but stronger than nomological necessity? 3a and 3b can be taken to express metaphysical necessity rather than logical necessity. Again, there are *de dicto/de re* issues in the neighborhood. But the truth of 3a and 3b are less obvious if we understand the necessity as metaphysical rather than logical. What does it mean to say that it is metaphysically necessary that all mortals soul-die or that all mortals metaphysically necessarily soul-die? Until we have a clear sense of the term *metaphysical* in this context, I'm not sure we have any grounds for judging the truth of 3a and 3b. Perhaps it is more plausible to say mortals metaphysically necessarily soul-die than to say that mortals logically necessarily soul-die. But upon what metaphysical principles might such a claim rest?

Perhaps some sense can be given to the term *metaphysical* in this context by noting that humans are contingent beings. They don't have to exist. But caution is called for here, for the claim about mortality is not that a mortal thing may not have existed. Mortal beings, once existing, are mortal, but not before they exist and not after they cease to exist. Contingency does not imply mortality, at least not all by itself. Once something exists, it may very well exist forever and still be contingent.

Perhaps, however, we can understand "metaphysical necessity" by appealing to the notion that once made, mortal things rely on something else—some metaphysical law or perhaps God's activity—to keep the mortal in existence. This could be a sort of sustaining contingency—once made, the continued existence of the thing is contingent on the application of the law or God's continued support. Once that law's application runs out or once God removes the ontological support needed for the mortal to continue, it ceases. One would then have to make out a case that God's sustaining activity or the metaphysical law simply stops applying to each and every mortal thing. I'll return to these matters below.

III

I move now beyond the concept of mortality to ways in which one might succumb to mortality; that is, to consider how one might soul-die. It's worth noting that it is possible for one to cease to exist as the person one is without the entirety of the being associated with one's self ceasing to exist. After all, one's body is part of oneself and yet one leaves it behind at death while one's consciousness—the "real" you—is presumably gone. Thus, mortality does not require the total cessation of all existence associated with one's self. What does it require? That is difficult to say in any detailed way.

Yet a general claim seems possible. Mortality coming to fruition, it might be said, requires only the cessation of existence of at least one feature that is essential for you to be what you are. To be what one is, the set of essential properties is separately necessary and jointly sufficient for one to exist. Obviously, the body's existence is not sufficient for a person, for the body remains—qua body—when one dies. Of course, a living body could be sufficient and necessary to avoid succumbing to mortality. But if it is just a body that is necessary then any body might do the trick. Perhaps a resurrected body might replace the old, non-living body and one would continue on in the upgraded model.

But what is essential to you as the individual you are or, more generally, as a member of the kind "human"? Which aspects of "you" need to cease to exist before one can (safely) be thought of as having succumbed to mortality? This is exceedingly hard to tell. Fortunately I don't need to answer that question in order to sort out the varieties of mortality that I want to discuss.

According to some understandings of the Christian doctrine of hell and some understandings of self-determination, the unredeemed lack self-determination. Some suggest that they are wholly stripped of any kind of agency (they can't do anything anymore, even if they maintain sinful dispositions that would manifest as sinful actions were they able to act). Others hold a somewhat weaker view, suggesting that because they are cut off from divine grace they are no longer free to act in any way other than in accord with sinful dispositions. That is, if the unredeemed have any free agency at all, it is of a wholly compatibilist character. But if (true) self-determination involves the ability to do otherwise than what one does—if it involves freedom in some more robust or libertarian sense—then the unredeemed no longer have self-determination according to traditional understandings of hell.

Now let's suppose that having libertarian free will is essential to being human, a point that is not an intellectual reach for a large number of Christian theologians and philosophers. Would those who have suffered the (permanent) loss of their libertarian free will have ceased to exist in the sense relevant to mortality as we've been considering it? Perhaps they have ceased to exist—mortality has overcome them—in that they no longer exist as members of the kind "human." Just as a dead human person leaves behind a body, so the unredeemed leave behind a conscious-but-less-than-free "soul," an entity that cannot truly be thought of as human for it lacks an essential property of being human. Or if the doctrine of the resurrection is true, then what is left behind at succumbing to mortality is a living animal organism but one that no longer is human in the relevant theological or philosophical sense. Whatever is left behind (after the loss of libertarian free will) no longer has all the essential features of being a human person and hence there isn't a sufficient set of characteristics for human personhood. The person has given way to mortality because the *human* is no more, having succumbed to mortality.

Here's another sort of case. Suppose in the afterlife what an individual loses is not (an essential-to-being-human) libertarian free will but a total loss of self-identifying memory. Unfortunately, similar things happen this side of death in those who fall prey to extreme cases of dementia or Alzheimer's. Clearly such folks have not succumbed to mortality in the sense I'm working with. But we do wonder whether they remain the same people they once were. They are, as we say, mere shadows of themselves. Now suppose there is an afterlife version of permanent self-identifying memory loss. Would one have succumbed to mortality even though one's consciousness continues on? I believe so. However here, it seems to me, the issue isn't that one no longer belongs in the kind "human" (although that may also be true) but that one is no longer the same individual person one once was. So instead of ceasing to have existence as a member of humankind, one ceases to exist as the individual, unique human one once was.

In both these cases, one loses something vital to one's existence as the thing one is. And, of course, the total nonexistence of consciousness itself will remove both free will (of any type) and self-identifying memory. But being conscious does not clearly require either free will or self-identifying memory. Nevertheless, we may be most comfortable in saying that with the permanent loss of consciousness (and here I speak not of comas from which one might return, even if the chances are negligibly slim, but I speak of final ontologically permanent loss of consciousness) we have ceased to exist. Still there do appear to be these other sorts of mortality. Consciousness might remain where one loses one's self-identifying memory, but it is no longer one's own consciousness. And consciousness might remain where one loses one's libertarian free will and it is replaced by a lesser sort of free will or perhaps by none at all, but one is then no longer a member of humankind. In the former case, the consciousness left behind is not one's own, for one has no sense of the (former) self one was. One has, so to speak, a clean slate of consciousness. In the latter case, one would (or could), presumably, continue to have the same consciousness but simply not be able to act in the way one formerly did. Either one would not be able to act at all (one no longer being an agent) or one would only be able to act according to a certain range of dispositions (sinful ones). But such a consciousness, even if continuous with the previous one, would not be a human consciousness. The human consciousness that was once yours has ceased to be a human consciousness.[14]

We might say, in cases such as the removal of free will or self-identifying memory, that upon mortality's success, one leaves behind one's consciousness rather like the dead leave behind their bodies. What was truly you—the you that has succumbed to mortality—leaves behind only a shadow of one's former self. To say one leaves one's consciousness behind is not to say that one has, post mortality, no consciousness at all. But the consciousness one keeps is not actually *human* consciousness, or at least the consciousness that was the individual human you were. But just as the body left behind is no longer living—no longer truly yours—so the consciousness left behind is no longer the same as the one had prior to one's succumbing to mortality. One has no less succumbed to mortality for having left that sort of consciousness behind. There is no existing human person to have a body or a consciousness. Either one has ceased to exist as the individual human person one was, or one has ceased to exist as a human altogether. In either case, one has succumbed to mortality.

There are, then, at least three sorts of mortality corresponding to the loss of various aspects of one's being: the loss of individual *personal* consciousness (locked to self-identifying memory), the loss of *human* consciousness (where consciousness continues, but in a non-human form), and the loss of consciousness simpliciter. But of course, the analysis depends on free will being an essential property of being human and self-identifying memory an essential property of being the individual one is. But if those

---

14. Babies and young children apparently lack libertarian freewill and hence won't count as human in the personal sense being used in the text. More care could be taken here and we might say that human children, unlike, perhaps, slugs or sea coral, have a natural capacity to develop libertarian free will given their actual biological structure. So the human baby, left to develop, will acquire libertarian free will, the damned will not.

features do not play the essential role I've assumed, perhaps others will and one will still end up with a variety of ways one can succumb to mortality.

It's worth noting before leaving this chapter that if what I've suggested is correct, the traditional notions of hell I described above are, in effect, annihilationist. Whether it is God or the human person herself who removes libertarian free will from the human person, the human person qua human is no more. The unredeemed human person—the human who sinned in an unforgiveable way—is destroyed and replaced by something that is not human. The unredeemed, so far as their (essential property of) libertarian free will is removed and replaced by something other than libertarian free will (whether a compatibilist free will or no free will at all), are no longer the people they once were for they are no longer human. As such, the punishment or torture of such folk (if what remains after mortality wins can be so-called) is morally unsanctionable insofar as the punishment is external—that is, coming from outside. Or there is, in effect, no punishment of the original person, for that person has ceased to exist having been annihilated by the change from one kind (human) to something else. Unless, of course, one counts cessation of existence itself as punishment. If so, it would have to be understood as a relational punishment, rather like we might understand succumbing to mortality as a relational loss. One is no longer there to feel the punishment, but the annihilation may be a loss nonetheless.[15]

---

15. Here we might return to Yourgrau and others who argue that succumbing to mortality is a loss even if it is a loss one can't feel.

CHAPTER 2

Varieties of Immortality

This chapter turns to immortality. Once again, there is a variety of immortalities even within the specific variety of personal immortality. Here the variety of immortalities discovered is not due to ways of coming into immortality (as one might come into mortality differently), but rather with the fact that immortality can be "sourced" in a variety of ways. Like mortality, immortality can be understood a number of ways.

4. To be immortal is to be such that one possibly doesn't soul-die.

5. To be immortal is to be such that one doesn't soul-die.

6. To be immortal is to be such that one necessarily doesn't soul-die.

These are parallel to 1 through 3 from the previous chapter and again one can interpret the claims in different ways. The first two can be covered fairly quickly. The first one, 4, suggests that immortality consists simply of the (logical) possibility that one never ceases to exist. It maps onto the notion of functional immortality discussed in chapter 1. Just because one doesn't cease to exist in a given possible world, it doesn't follow that there is no possible world in which the same object ceases to exist. The possibility that one doesn't soul-die just is the possibility that, in fact, one doesn't soul-die. This account doesn't seem strong enough to capture what we typically think of as immortality.

The second claim, 5, parallels 2 in its nomological structure. Immortality would consist in the fact that immortals in appropriate conditions fall under the relevant natural laws. As such they continue to exist. Once again, however, this would depend on soul-death being, in effect, physical death as it is difficult to see how natural laws would apply to a non-physical soul-death.

The final version has both a *de dicto* and a *de re* understanding. Where "I" is "is immortal," "S": is "soul-dies" and "□" is "logically necessary that," and "~" is "it is not the case that," we get

6a. □(x)(Ix→~Sx) Necessarily, if x is immortal, it is not the case that x soul-dies.

6b. (x)(Ix→□~Sx) If x is immortal, then necessarily it is not the case that x soul-dies.

The *de dicto* reading tells us that something cannot be immortal without also continuing to exist forever while the *de re* reading tells us that an immortal thing is necessarily such that it exists without ceasing. The latter claim suggests that immortals have the property of existing without cessation in every possible world. In other words, a lack of soul-death is an essential property of immortals.

Here an interesting feature of immortality emerges. Recall that the term *mortality* applies to a thing only so long as it exists. It doesn't apply to it before it exists nor after it ceases to exist, at least not strictly. The reason for this feature is that something that doesn't exist cannot cease to exist. So strictly speaking, "immortality" applies only to existing things as well. But a second feature is true of the term *immortal*. Immortality appears to be a property one can't lose. If one loses one's immortality (as one might in functional immortality) one was never truly immortal in the first place. This gives one a reason to think that neither 4 nor 5 will work as an account of immortality. The former only gives one functional immortality and the latter an accidental immortality. I want to leave functional immortality on the table, but there is some pressure here to move us toward taking 6 as the best understanding of immortality.

But again, we face a choice between understanding "necessity" to mean logical or metaphysical necessity. Of course, if immortality is an essential feature of a thing, it cannot lose that property and still exist. Because immortality is a property one can't lose, being immortal entails that one continues to exist forever. Does it follow that immortality is an essential property of a thing that has it? No. Here we might rely on a metaphysical sense of necessity. To get at that sense, we might turn to Tom Morris, who introduces various modal notions that are not essential or merely accidental. In particular, I'm interested in what he calls an "immutable property."

Some properties are temporary, that is, an individual begins to have a property, exemplifies it for a while, and then ceases to have it. But, Morris continues:

> It may happen, for example, that an individual has a property which it cannot cease to have. Let us refer to such a case as one of an enduring property. Likewise, it is conceivable that an object have a property which it cannot have begun to have. We shall call this an immemorial property. Finally, a property which is both enduring and immemorial will be characterized as immutable. An immutable property is such that the individual having it cannot have begun to have it and cannot cease to have it. We can call any property which is immemorial or enduring or immutable a stable property. . . . The mere fact that an entity has a property which in fact it never began to have and never will cease to have is not enough for that property to count as immemorial or enduring by our definitions. The modal element in each definition should indicate that with the notion of a stable property we are concerned with something more than the mere *de facto* histories of property bearers.[1]

Stable properties, continues Morris, need to be separated from the essential/accidental or necessary/contingent classifications. An individual could exist without a given stable property, but not without its essential properties.

But Morris makes a further important distinction: "A property can be immemorial, enduring, or immutable in either a weak or a strong sense. A property is weakly enduring for an individual just in case that individual has the property, and there can be no time during the individual's existence when it will have ceased to have that property. It is strongly enduring just in case it is exemplified and there can be no time at which the individual ceases to have it."[2] Further, a property "is weakly immemorial for an individual just in case the individual has the property, and there can have been no time during the individual's existence after which it began to have that property. It is strongly immemorial just in case it is exemplified and there can have been no time at which its bearer began to exemplify it."[3] There are parallel weak and strong versions of immutable properties—weak if both weakly enduring and immemorial, strong if both strongly enduring and immemorial.

1. Morris, "Properties, Modalities, and God," 36.
2. Ibid., 37.
3. Ibid., 38.

He continues on to note that it may appear that only necessary beings have strongly enduring or immemorial properties, but that is not so. Consider a being which "(1) in fact exists, and either (2) could not have begun to exist, or (3) cannot cease to exist but (4) could have failed to exist at all."[4] Such a being would be contingent because of (4) but either (2) or (3) be true. Its existence would be either strongly enduring or strongly immemorial and hence it would be capable of having strongly enduring or immemorial properties. But on the notion of immortality as I've laid it out above, a being that has (1), (3), and (4) would be contingent but immortal. Its having the property of "existence" would itself be a strongly enduring property. Once existing, in other words, it could not cease to exist. So immortality would be an enduring property—the property of existing forever (not capable of soul-death) once natal (existing). Nevertheless, immortality is not an essential property, for God could have made humans without it.

Morris also says that an individual could satisfy both conditions (2) and (3) in which case that individual would have strongly immutable existence. An example of this would be a number having the property of being prime. There is no time at which it ceases to be prime and no time at which it becomes prime. In both cases, it is the way it is because numbers are timeless. This goes beyond immortality, however. All that is required for immortality is that once one exists, one always exists.

Now this raises all sorts of questions about the why or how a thing has an immutable property. I'll return to this issue below. First, however, I want to explore the Christian view of the afterlife that has come to be called "annihilationism" and the account of immortality behind it known as "conditional immortality." A conditionalist is someone who believes that humans are mortal when created but can be granted immortality by God at the final judgment. A redeemed human is granted a new property, a property that heretofore she didn't have—immortality.

There are three ways to understand conditional immortality, although I'll retain the term "conditional immortality" to refer to the basic idea. The first understanding I'll call "essentialist conditional immortality." Here humans are both created mortal and have mortality essentially. The redeemed, however, are granted a change in nature after judgment. What was naturally (essentially) mortal becomes naturally (essentially) immortal. Such a change is surely problematic for it requires a change in kind and the individual ceases to be the individual it was. An essential property is a property

4. Ibid., 40.

one must have to exist as the thing one is. If one must have the property of being mortal to be human, then becoming immortal rules out staying the same kind of thing. Taking on immortality would thus cause one to cease being human. Would the resulting being (if such a change were indeed possible) be the same human who, say, developed a saving relationship with God while on earth? No, for the new and improved being would no longer be human. If this is what those who propose conditional immortality mean, it's not clear that it is possible. Nothing can change essentially and remain the same sort of thing it is. In fact, to lose any essential property is to cease to exist as the thing one is. Essentialist conditional immortality as an understanding of conditional immortality holds no hope of success.

But a second understanding is possible. I'll call it "enduring conditional immortality." Here humans are created mortal where mortality is an accidental property. At the judgment, the redeemed are granted immortality as a strongly enduring property. All essential properties are enduring properties but not all enduring properties are also essential. One cannot lose the property of "once having had hair" (while existing), but that property is not essential, although it is weakly enduring. It might have been the case that one never had hair. Likewise, with the immortality one takes on (by, say, God's grace). Once one has it, one cannot lose it; in this case, however, it is a strongly enduring property. To say one has immortality of this sort includes saying that one once was (in fact) mortal or could have been (if God didn't give you immortality at natality) mortal.

A third option I'll call "functional conditional immortality." On this understanding, humans are by nature mortal (where mortality is an essential property of being human) but for the redeemed God grants a (permanent) "stay of cessation." Although humans remain mortal, they are sustained forever in their mortality. Mortality on such an understanding would revert to 1b. One's soul-death would merely be a logical possibility and neither a fact (as of yet) nor a necessary fact about oneself. Functional immortality—and one might hesitate to call such a true immortality for reasons noted above—presumably comes from "outside" the human person. The picture is that humans are naturally inclined to nothingness but are sustained in existence forever as mortals by the "outside" power of divine grace. That is not to say that humans would not be changed at judgment into something better than we currently are, but just that God does not change human essential nature from mortal to immortal, or one's accidental mortality to a strongly enduring immortality. This view gives us immortality in the sense of everlastingness, but that everlastingness is not actually part of human nature. It is due entirely to God's sustaining activity.

Note that enduring conditional immortality needs further work as well in explaining how it is that a human could have the strongly enduring property of immortality. One is tempted to say that one is granted an enduring property by some outside power. Such immortality is not obviously intrinsic to humans for they need not have been created with it. To be human, they need not have the property of immortality. Whence the property then? Like functional immortality, it appears that its source must be external to it. However, because it is a strongly enduring property, not even God can cause it to be removed from a human. Having said that, however, it may turn out that humans have immortality because they have some other property.

After a very interesting discussion of divine sinlessness, Morris writes the following:

> It seems that we have here an instance of an extrinsically stable property. It is not obvious that sinlessness is stable for God in virtue of being essential to him. Nor is it an intrinsically stable property. Our arguments seem to indicate that it can be viewed as a property whose stability is conferred on it by the nature of its bearer, or by other properties exemplified by its bearer.[5]

I will propose below that human immortality is also extrinsic to humans, a property conferred on humans by other properties we have. That fact about humans entails that conditional immortality is not a successful understanding of the afterlife. But it is also extrinsic in another sense as well, the sense in which God need not have created humans in the first place. Having done so, however, God cannot destroy us. A sketch of this is found in chapter 3, but the details will await chapter 5.

In addition to these three views, there is natural immortality. Humans might be essentially immortal from our creation. This sort of immortality is not just a property one cannot lose or a strongly enduring property, although it is that too. Rather, this sort of property is essential to being human. If we are by nature immortal then not even God could destroy us, once created, and not only the redeemed but the unredeemed will exist forever. Natural immortality can provide grounds for the eternal-conscious-punishment view of hell and, if we believe many of those who argue for soul cessationism, natural immortality (of a Hellenistic sort) played just that

5. Ibid., 54.

role historically. But natural immortality does not itself entail everlasting conscious punishment. It could also provide grounds for universalism, the view that ultimately everyone is redeemed. Natural immortality is neutral in that regard. The same is true of strongly enduring immortality, if it is something given us at our natality—in other words, if the property of immortality is immutable.

The annihilationists depend on the notion that being mortal (prior to judgment, at any rate) allows God the moral and metaphysical space to simply let us cease to be of our own choice or at God's command. But we need to say more of mortality and it is important to do so in order to avoid a potential confusion between contingency and mortality. Whether we humans have natural, strongly enduring, or conditional immortality (of any type), we remain contingent. We didn't have to be. Yet in each of the three cases, the manner in which we are sustained is different. Here we might think of abstract objects. There are a variety of views about the relationship between God and abstract objects and I won't go into details here. But it seems that if God is the fundamental existent on which everything else depends, abstract objects, even though they have always existed—they are necessities or at least stable entities—still depend on God's existence at least logically. In short: no God, no abstract objects. Indeed, no God, nothing at all. The difference between abstract objects and naturally immortal humans is that the former have existed so long as God has (or perhaps atemporally, as God might be), whereas humans came into existence at some point and then continue on forever (temporally). Both things—naturally immortal humans and abstract objects—are contingent in that without God, neither would exist. The difference is there never was a time when abstract objects were not, whereas there was a time when humans were not.

What of the contingency of humans when understood as conditionally immortal? We must divide and conquer at this point. For functional immortality, it seems that not only was there a time when humans were not, but that for any human at any given time they could possibly cease to be. This is true because humans don't have either the essential or the strongly enduring property of immortality. Is this a more radical type of contingency (if one may so speak) than what is true of abstract objects or naturally immortal humans? It would seem so, at least at first blush. If humans are naturally immortal, they seem, as Socrates might have put it, "like the forms" and can't cease to be (once made). If they are functionally immortal, then in principle they could cease to be, should God choose that course of action. That's what "being mortal" means.

For strongly enduring immortality, I've already suggested that it seems to be an extrinsic property and would, as such, at least rely on the presence of some other property humans have. Perhaps it relies on God directly, however, and is not mediated by another property. In that case, although it is property humans can't lose, it would be so because God supports a situation in which humans have it and yet it is something short of an essential property.

What if immortality were essential to humans? We would, of course, be contingent. Our everlasting existence, however, would not be something God could override, once God created us, perhaps in a manner similar to the way in which God can't bring about the end of the necessities. Our existence would be something not even God could cause to cease in that it would flow, somehow, from God logically (and not just causally).

CHAPTER 3

Can God Cause Humans to Cease to Exist?

Annihilationism in Christian eschatology denies that humans are immortal from natality. That is, it denies that humans are, once created, essentially or enduringly immortal. Hence it denies that humans cannot come to an end. Annihilationism is often explicated via conditional immortality. Conditional immortality has two theoretical components. The first is that humans are mortal. The second is that the redeemed human is granted immortality at bodily death or sometime after. Meanwhile, the unredeemed are left or caused to cease existence whether by following their own proclivities toward non-being or by an act of God. In short, all humans are mortal initially and only some—the redeemed—are granted immortality.[1] Immortality is thus conditional on redemption.

I want to reflect in this chapter on the possibility of annihilationism and hence will focus only on what is necessary for that view. I'm particularly interested in the claim that humans are mortal. I make no attempt at present to consider the second component of conditional immortality—the immortality of the redeemed or immortality's nature. Are there philosophical grounds for the mortality of the human person, and what might they be?

We saw in chapter 1 that mortality can be understood in a variety of ways. The main options for understanding mortality are that mortals possibly soul-die, that mortals nomologically necessarily soul-die, that mortals logically necessarily soul-die, and that mortals metaphysically necessarily

---

1. For a substantial number of essays on conditional immortality and annihilationism see Date, Stump, and Anderson, eds., *Rethinking Hell*; and Date and Highfield, *A Consuming Passion*, 247.

soul-die. I suggested that the view that mortals nomologically necessarily soul-die would apply to the human body but that soul-death, should it be of something beyond the body, would not fall under natural laws. I also suggested that understanding human mortality to be a logically necessary feature of humans seems too strong. Surely there is a possible world in which humans are immortal.

Of the other two, the thought that mortals possibly soul-die is quite weak. It claims only that a given mortal may or may not soul-die. In one way, it's this notion that I'm working with in this chapter, for it is asking the question whether it is within God's moral power to cause a human to cease existence. I provide the best argument I can come up with to show that it is within God's moral purview to cause humans to cease to exist. But God's moral purview is not the same as whether it is logically possible for God to cause permanent human cessation.

In another sense, however, I am dealing with mortality understood as the metaphysical necessity of soul-death. If it is morally permissible for God to bring about soul-death for humans, then it seems that it also is metaphysically possible for God to bring about soul-death. We all know that "ought" implies "can." But does "moral permissibility" also imply "can"? That is certainly not true for humans. There are lots of times one morally can do something without that implying that one metaphysically can. What of God? Since God is omnipotent, it seems that God can do, with the exception of the logically impossible, anything. Recall in chapter 1 that I suggested that perhaps we can understand "metaphysical necessity" by appealing to the notion that once made, mortal things rely on something else—some metaphysical law or perhaps God's activity—to keep the mortal in existence. This could be a sort of sustaining contingency—once made, the continued existence of the thing is contingent on the application of the law or God's continued support. Once that law's application runs out or once God removes the ontological support needed for the mortal to continue, it ceases. One would then have to make out a case that God's sustaining activity or the metaphysical law simply stops being applied (God) or applying (law) to each and every mortal thing.

So here we might consider whether there are conditions under which God's supporting power can be withdrawn from humans. Those conditions, we might propose, are moral conditions. Thus, if it is morally permissible for God to cause or allow the cessation of human persons then there are conditions under which humans can cease to be. That, however, only gives us metaphysical possibility, not necessity. But if God needs no moral reason at all for bringing about the end of human persons but there is some more deeply rooted metaphysical reason why God could bring us all to an end, then the entire immortality discussion may simply be an empty one. Immortality would ultimately just be a sort of functional immortality. God could in principle end it at any time.

One way to defend the view that humans are mortal is to suggest that because we humans are made entirely by God that the divinity owns us. As the complete property of God, it is in the moral purview of the divinity to allow or cause the permanent cessation of any human. Because God can allow or bring about the permanent end of humans, it follows that they are mortal. But note that when I say that it is within God's moral purview to destroy humans, I am not necessarily saying that God has a moral reason to destroy humans. It would be morally permissible for God to destroy us just because God wants to do so.

To explore that argument, section I presents the basic soul-cessation argument. Section II considers various arguments that support, on the one hand, and undercut, on the other, the soul-cessation argument. Section III takes the results of the discussion and advocates for immortality (understood either as an enduring property or an essential one), thus undermining annihilationism.

I

Socrates once argued that we ought not to commit suicide because it militates against humans being owned by the gods. While not stated, Socrates's argument presumes that it is up to the gods when one ought to die. Socrates, of course, thought the (separable, dualistic) soul immortal and death nothing more than the separation of the soul from the body. One could not, on Socratic grounds, commit soul-suicide and bring to an end one's soulish being. Or at least so one presumes, given Socrates's discussion of the afterlife in the *Phaedo*.

If we humans are, in fact, owned by God—and leaving aside Socrates's arguments for immortality—is that grounds enough for the divinity to be able to bring about the permanent end of the human soul? Consider the following, what I'll call "the soul-cessation argument."

Can God Cause Humans to Cease to Exist?

- A. Anything fully owned by person p can be caused to cease to exist by p with moral impunity. (Premise)
- B. Any human soul is owned by God. (Premise)
- C. Therefore, it is within God's moral purview to cause any human soul to cease to exist. (A, B)

This argument assumes that if something is within God's moral purview that the divinity can, in metaphysical fact, accomplish the deed. I will not defend this assumption beyond what I said in this chapter's opening remarks. We should note, further, that even were this argument successful, its conclusion is limited. C only claims that God has a right to destroy human souls. That right may very well be overridden by other factors. Perhaps God loves the soul so much that even though the divinity has the right to destroy the soul, God never does. If we want to conclude that soul-cessation is possible, we'll have to say more. So perhaps we need to add this further argument:

- D. God has no reason not to take up the divine right to cause the cessation of a human soul. (Premise)
- E. If it is within God's moral purview to cause any human soul to cease to exist and God has no reason not to take up the divine right to cause the cessation of a human soul, God can allow or cause the cessation of any human soul. (Premise)
- F. Therefore, any soul can be allowed or caused to cease existence. (C, D, E)

This argument is quite broad, for it suggests both that any soul can cease to be and that God has no reason not to allow or cause such cessation. In other words, this is a defense of mortality in general and not merely for the recalcitrant unredeemed. So it would apply, if successful, even to the redeemed who, on conditional immortality, are thought to be immortal. If it were successful, it appears that the conditionalist would have to say that although redeemed humans remain mortal they never cease to exist because God permanently sustains them. In other words, God would only provide for functional immorality for the redeemed and God moment-to-moment overrides their natural tendency to cessation and does so entirely from the divine side.

It may seem obvious that God does have reasons not to allow or cause the cessation of human souls. Love, as I mentioned above, is the prime candidate. Does love give God a reason to override the divine right to the cessation of human souls? An affirmative answer is by no means obvious. Let's consider a strong version of annihilationist Calvinism. A Calvinist of this persuasion may suggest that God doesn't love the unredeemed souls. Could this be why they cease to be permanently? No. One cannot turn the observation that God doesn't love the unredeemed into the reason that they are unredeemed. On Calvinist grounds, we all deserve annihilation. It is our sin that condemns us and the unredeemed are condemned not by the fact that God doesn't love them, but by their sin. Now it is true, according to Calvinism, that God saves only those the divinity chooses. But it is also true that God does so for no reason we can tell. So love cannot be the reason God overrides the divine right to allow or cause human cessation.

The Arminian soul-cessationist is on no firmer footing than the Calvinist. On Arminian grounds, the unredeemed are bound toward annihilation because they freely reject God's offer of love. God loves the unredeemed, but the divinity's hands are tied by human rejection of that love. Here it might be suggested that God loves humans and therefore has a reason to override the divine right to human cessation. Unfortunately, the reason to override is itself overridden by recalcitrant human free rejection of God's love. Here it appears that God has a defeated reason to override the divine right to allow or cause our cessation. A defeated reason is as good, functionally, as no reason at all.

More generally, although love seems like a good candidate to overthrow God's right to bring about the cessation of human beings, love might just as well lead God to soul-euthanasia for the unredeemed. Eternal conscious punishment seems, as it is often pointed out, far too great for the sorts of sins humans commit; the proportionality argument is powerful against it. Wouldn't it be better—more loving—if God could just allow or cause the permanent cessation of the recalcitrant unredeemed? So although there is some reason to think God would not allow or cause soul-cessation, it's not clear that it is sufficient by itself.

III

The soul-cessation argument has in its favor the intuition that attaches to private property ownership as granting something's owner total control over that thing. There are, of course, exceptions. One's use of one's property cannot harm others—one cannot pollute one's land because that pollution harms others. One's use of private property cannot interfere with another's use of her private property—building a fence so high that one's neighbor can't see the cars coming down the street when pulling out of her drive, for example. But the obvious difference between these earthy examples and the case of God's possible ownership of humans is that God is sovereign and as such we need not worry about whether the divine's use of the created order conflicts with someone's interest in the results.[2]

To help us discern the strength of the soul-cessation argument, consider this parallel argument. I'll refer to it as the "painting argument."

G. Any painting fully made by a painter is fully owned by the painter. (Premise)

H. Anything fully owned by person p can be caused to cease to exist by p with moral impunity. (Premise)

I. Therefore, it is morally acceptable for a painter to make a painting and then destroy it. (G, H)

The painting argument seems sound. Its driving idea is that creative work and material objects used in the creative work (when duly purchased or retrieved from the common property by the artist) are completely at her disposal to do with as she will. This follows directly from our sense of private property ownership. The only exceptions to H (or A from the soul-cessation argument, which is identical) occur when harm comes to some other person by the destruction of the owned object or when the object is used to interfere with someone else's rights. In the case of God, as I've noted, there may simply be no harms that come from the destruction of the soul, given God's sovereignty.

But not all is sugar and cream here. Let's assume, as isn't hard for the theist, that the world is inherently normative. That is, value is part of the

---

2. There may be another argument hidden here on the side of the anti-soul-cessationist, viz., the cessation of a soul may very well affect other human persons and so God may need to keep everyone in hell in existence because their permanent deaths will cause pain for those, say, in heaven who remember and love them. This topic may come to the forefront in discussion of heaven where it is claimed that there will be no more tears. That may imply that grief does not exist in heaven. Or it may turn up in descriptions of heaven and divine judgment such as can be found in Jonathan Edwards where the redeemed are looking over the parapets of heaven and rejoicing that those in hell below are receiving their just desserts, a scene that I find rather distasteful, if not unconscionable.

structure of the world and is not, fundamentally, something created by humans. Even given that assumption, however, some value may be social and cultural creation and we might say that when something is valuable but merely culturally so, destroying it may be bad, but the badness exists only within the cultural context. However, when something is valuable not merely for cultural reasons but for structural reasons we might say destroying it is bad objectively. The question is, is destroying the painting culturally or objectively bad? Is there something deep in the nature of moral relationships holding between individuals and their created objects, something beyond mere social construct?

Arguably, when a particular thing is structurally valuable, it is valuable because it stands in a certain relationship with the normative world. Plato might have said that an action is just because it participates in justice. In contemporary terms, we are more likely to speak of a just action instantiating justice. If we assume justice is part of the normative structure of the world, the just act is just because of the objective nature of justice. When Agent A instantiates justice on a particular occasion we say that A is responsible for the act. And when we want someone to take responsibility for an action, we sometimes even say that we want the agent to "own" the action. Now this use of "own" is metaphorical, derived likely from more standard uses of the term *own* in private property situations. No one literally owns the just action. But there is another reason to think the private ownership model is misplaced here. Because a just action instantiates justice, and because justice is something we all have an interest in, a just action in some sense could be said to belong to all of us. That is because justice, by its very nature, is communal—it is structurally related to each and every person. Indeed, I think a case can be made that all value terms are communal in this sense.

Consider a beautiful ocean scene, the sun slowly sinking below the rock formations that line stretches of beach in Oregon, shadows playing on the waves, a brilliant pattern of scattered clouds. Suppose this scene moves a person to ask "Isn't that beautiful?" The question is meant to draw agreement, to call attention to something of worth in which we all share. No one owns beauty any more than anyone owns justice. Similarly with truth. The announcement that p is true is expected to be agreed with—given the proposition's truth. Of course, one can ask whether p is in fact true—that is an epistemological question. But the actual truth of p—the metaphysics of the situation—doesn't belong to anyone or, perhaps better, the value attributed to p when it is true is shared by one and all. Truth is communal in that sense, just as are justice, goodness, and beauty.

The nature of these values is that they are shared and not personally owned. Let's call such values structural values. They are structured by the world. Consider, then, the painting-structural-value argument.

a. Causing something with structural value to cease to exist is bad. (Premise)

b. Premise a. is true even if the object in question is created entirely by a given maker. (Premise)

c. Beautiful paintings are structurally valuable. (Premise)

d. Therefore, a painter causing her own beautiful painting to cease existing is a bad thing. (a, b, c)

If the painting-structural-value argument is correct, then there may be a problem with the painting argument. Structural value cannot be owned. That is not to say no one can own a painting in a legal sense, but such ownership is a social, legal construct. Perhaps one might even say that one can own a painting in a moral sense,[3] but it seems that in both the legal and the moral ownership cases, the ownership is nothing more than an important cultural construct. At the deepest level of structural value, the value in which the world is imbedded, beauty and its instantiations are owned by no one. So although a painter may legally and morally own a painting, she doesn't own its beauty. If she destroys it, she is doing a bad thing.

There are other issues to consider as well. The first premise—premise a—is very powerful. Suppose one concludes that a piece of Oregon oceanfront is particularly beautiful—structurally beautiful. Would it then be morally wrong to build a road through it down to the beach? This question points out the need to specify any limits on premise a. To know whether the painting-structural-value argument works one must decide certain things. First, is the painting under consideration actually beautiful? More generally, when one applies this sort of argument in different circumstances, one must consider when and under what conditions something is beautiful, just, true, and so forth. Second, does such value ever override the rights of private property ownership? Third, when is the structural value of a thing

---

3. Even here I'm not sure that it is true that a painter can morally own a beautiful painting any more than one can say that one owns a just action. One is responsible for it, but one doesn't own it.

great enough (if ever) to override private property rights, rights that seem to entail that an owner can do anything to a piece of private property—even destroy it—so long as no one else is being harmed? And to return us to the original and most important question, are private property rights something deep in the nature of moral relationships holding between individuals and their created objects? Are private property rights indeed structural and objective or cultural and merely constructed?

Let's grant temporarily that a given painting is, indeed, beautiful and that it is beautiful enough to override private property rights and that private property ownership is something more than a mere cultural construct. Why would it be bad to destroy the painting? We have, it seems, two deeply conflicting types of value, a moral value (private property ownership) and a metaphysical value (beauty—in this instance). The contrast between these two sorts of value—moral and metaphysical—may allow us to judge the action moral, but bad. How bad the act is will depend on how beautiful the painting is and on whether there are other mitigating circumstances. The same would be true of putting a road through the beautiful piece of Oregon coast property. Such actions might still be bad even if morally justified.

The critic of the painting argument might press the following. If the painting-structural-value argument is correct, the painting argument fails, for premise G is false. It is false because premises a and b are true intuitively.

Intuition, however, will not win the day here. Others may have conflicting intuitions and thus just disagree. We need to ask, then, whether we have anything other than intuition on which to base a decision about whether a and b are true.

We can at least say that the third requirement listed above is very important. Is there a threshold of value a thing may have structurally such that even the thing's creator would be morally wrong to destroy it? On the one hand, it seems within the maker's moral purview to destroy anything she makes, no matter how much value it has structurally. She does, after all, *own* the object in question. On the other hand, structural value may not be something that can be privately held. That is, structurally valuable things, even if owned by their maker, are the sorts of objects that ought not be destroyed, but rather to continue existing for all to enjoy. When we think of structural value we are thinking of value which is by nature shared and universally so, including shared by God. A made thing's structural value does not obviously lie within the maker's moral control, once made. It would be bad if the structurally valuable thing ceased to be; and because of the badness of the cessation of the thing itself, it would be morally wrong for anyone to (intentionally) cause it to cease existence (all other things being equal). But even with these observations, it seems that we are left with conflicting intuitions and these conflicting intuitions are not easy to clear up. How much structural value does a thing need to be outside morally acceptable control of its maker?

In the end, that depends on how we understand the answer to the forth question, viz., whether private property is something deep in the nature of moral relationships holding between individuals and their created objects.

IV

The soul-cessation argument and the painting argument seem to rise and fall together. However, there are important differences. Consider the human-structural-value argument:

- e. Causing something with structural value to cease to exist is bad. (Premise)
- f. Premise e. is true even if the object in question is created entirely by a given maker. (Premise)
- g. Humans are structurally valuable. (Premise)
- h. Therefore, God's causing the soul-cessation of humans, even though God created them, is a bad thing. (e, f, g)

When we attempt to apply to humans the sort of reasoning found in the painting-structural-value argument, one might first ask whether God owns humans—or can own humans—in the same way an artist owns her painting. Humans are, after all, free. No human can own (morally) another human, but humans can own paintings. Can God own humans?

If one takes a strong enough view of the value of human (libertarian) self-determination so that the value of self-determination is structural, then God doesn't own us. Suppose, for example, it were true of humans that we had the sort of free will and self-determination captured by Robert Kane. He defines the freedom of self-determination as "the power or ability to act of your own free will in the sense of a will (character, motives, and purposes) of your own making—a will that you yourself, to some degree, were ultimately responsible for forming."[4] He then suggests that this sort of

4. Kane, *Free Will*, 172.

freedom presupposes a further incompatibilist freedom, viz., the freedom of self-formation, which is "the power to form one's own will in a manner that is undetermined by one's past by virtue of will-setting or self-forming actions . . . over which one has plural voluntary control."[5] By the phrase "plural voluntary control," Kane has in mind the following: "[A]gents are able to bring about whichever of the options they will, when they will to do so, for the reasons they will to do so, on purpose, rather than accidentally or by mistake, without being coerced or compelled in doing so or in willing to do so, or otherwise controlled in doing or in willing to do so by any other agents or mechanisms."[6] If humans can so determine their character and their choices, it seems that the ownership of such a person is simply ruled out on moral grounds. Otherwise God would be morally free to coerce us into obedience and salvation either by determining our characters or overriding a given choice we make.

But perhaps a case can be made that God does own us. Consider that we wouldn't exist at all save for God's creating us. Christians standardly hold that we humans owe God allegiance and worship. Perhaps the owing of allegiance and worship indicates that God owns us. So perhaps the sense of ownership is stronger with God than, say, with a painter and her painting. Some issues to consider here include the following. First, perhaps "ownership" is just the wrong term. The notion of private property ownership, although widely held, is a newcomer to the scene and it is by no means the only option. Usufruct rights are another, or a Marxist construal of common ownership. Or perhaps even more relevant, there is the biblical notion of stewardship. Second, if we are owned by God, it could be argued that we are owned in a way distinct from private property ownership. The creation of the world by God is different in important ways from the creation of an artwork by an artist. We owe our being not merely to God's creative work with pre-existing material objects, but the very material of which we are made is brought into being by God out of nothing. So if we are owned by God it is an ownership for which the owned should be grateful. The entire notion of sin as rebellion relies on a special relationship between God and humanity. Indeed, Scripture indicates that all of creation worships God—as Jesus enters Jerusalem on the donkey we are told that even the stones will cry out, if the people do not. And, of course, Scripture

---

5. Ibid.
6. Ibid., 173.

is laden with references to Christians being slaves of Christ. The alternative is, indeed, to be a slave to sin or the devil. As Bob Dylan says, "you gotta serve somebody."

But perhaps the most potent observation is that since God made us out of nothing it is morally acceptable for God to return us, so to speak, to nothing. This intuition is rooted, perhaps, in the sense that when God creates us, any value we have is derivative from God. Since God is sovereign, there is nothing in principle wrong with God's simply destroying not only humans, but all of creation should God decide to do so. God would, on those grounds, need no reason to destroy all of creation. God owes us nothing.

So which is it: does God own humans or not? Perhaps we can settle our uneasy intuitions in this way. Every structurally valuable thing is valuable because of its nature. Beautiful paintings are structurally valuable because they are beautiful. The individual beauty of the painting is created by the painter and, in a fairly straight-forward sense, remains in the control of the artist. Beauty is not self-determining, one might suggest, and therefore the instantiation of beauty is in the control of its maker. The nature of some structurally valuable things, however, are automatically outside the control of the maker because the maker creates them to be self-determining. Humans are the best case in point. Whether something's structural value overrides its creator's right to destroy it may depend, then, not on structural value per se, but on the *type* of structural value a thing has. That, in turn, will depend on the nature of the thing itself.

The main reason humans have structural value, we might surmise, is that we are morally responsible because we are self-determining things. One can construct a plausible argument based on human free will against the notion that God can cause or allow permanent human cessation. The argument runs, briefly, along these lines. Humans have metaphysical value because of robust free will. Robust free will makes possible the increase of metaphysical value in the universe, part of God's plan. God's plan cannot be logically separated from God's essence and nothing God does or allows can undermine God's essence. Thus, not even God can destroy or allow the destruction of human souls, once created. God can't destroy or allow the cessation of human souls not simply because God has a moral obligation, but because humans are structurally valuable in their own right. Based on that sort of argument, even if one's intuitions are that God as creator can destroy the valuable things coming from the divine hand in general, the line is drawn at humans. Their way of being structurally good is rooted in their nature, a nature that self-determines. I'll return to explain and defend this argument at length in chapter 5. For now I'm content to say that there's nothing new in the observation that self-determination is highly valuable. That observation has been used to diffuse some versions of the problem of evil since at least Augustine. When God placed human free agents in the world, God risked the horrendous quality and quantity of evil that followed from that placement. Of course, that alone doesn't show that the instantiation of free will is so important that God cannot morally destroy it. Also, the particular issue with hell is not merely the existence of evil that will someday end, but rather that the evils of hell continue forever. Wouldn't it be better if God simply caused all the suffering souls to cease existence? But if free will is enough to bear the burden of horrendous earthly evils, is it enough to bear the forever evil of hell? Perhaps free will is *so* valuable that even though it is attached to such a horrible existence God cannot morally destroy humans. God must therefore keep the recalcitrant unredeemed in existence forever. If God's hands are morally tied by human free resistance to God's offer of salvation, and God cannot morally destroy recalcitrant unredeemed folk, then hell must have inhabitants so long as those in hell decide not to exit it by turning toward God in a blessed relationship. Because God loves humans and respects our freely made decisions and actions, God keeps hell in existence. But is God's love for us enough to justify continued human existence in hell? Why not the opposite? God's love may be enough to end our misery permanently.

It is important to clearly distinguish between the choices we make with free will and the fact that we have free will. But what is it that God values about free will? Is it the choices we make with it or the fact that we have it? The structural value of free will could rest in one of two places, and when one says that God values free will, it may matter which of the two resting places one has in mind. On the one hand, there is the property "being free" as instantiated in a human person. On the other hand, there are the actual, concrete choices that having the capacity supports. So one has the capacity to choose freely and one also has the actual choice made. So, for example, a given human may have, at the last judgment, the ability to choose either redemption or continued disobedience. That same human, once having made the choice can be said to have acted freely. Let's call the first of these "freedom-as-capacity" and the second "freedom-as-choice." Which is it that God values most, freedom-as-capacity or freedom-as-choice? Insofar as humans make bad choices, surely God is unhappy. But since God was willing to risk such bad choices, originally unleashing sin and death into the world, God must be willing to accept any and all freedom-as-choice resulting from our freedom-as-capacity.

That is only part of the story, however. Surely if God knew ahead of time that humans would make the world unredeemable by using their freedom-as-capacity to make bad choices, then God wouldn't have created the world. The redeemable world God makes has built into it God's ability to overcome all evil. So God's willingness to risk our freedom-as-choice when it leads to evil is rooted in God's own goodness and not, in fact, some sort of overall goodness vs. badness that humans might bring about in their free will. But that is a way of saying that the value of free will lies not in the choices we make using it, but in *the free will itself*—the freedom-as-capacity.

Here we can say something further about the structural value of free will. God, being free in the divine creative love, creates a world. Genesis says that the world God made is good, and when humans enter, that it is very good. The created order is an order structured by value. Theists resist naturalism because they can't see how values can be deeply embedded in a world without God. But they also use the central value of human free will—and in particular robust libertarian versions of it—to claim that evil has an explanation not due to God. The choices humans made led to evil in the world. Yet God gave humans that have freedom. Why? Not so freedom could be used toward evil ends, but because we humans are made in God's image and that image is what allows for love. Freedom-as-capacity is itself valuable. In God, of course, the divine freedom is tied to the divine love. God's freedom is not the freedom to do evil, but to choose among the large and creative range of ways of making more value in the universe. God's freedom-as-capacity is tied to God's always positive, always loving, freedom-as-choice. God's freedom is always for the good.

Not so with humans. Although we have the very valuable freedom-as-capacity, we can use that capacity for ill. God respects, of course, our choices, even the bad ones, but only in the sense that God allows them to occur. The divinity does not respect our bad choices in the valuational sense. It is only when we humans use our freedom-as-capacity for good ends that God respects them in the valuational sense.

Are there choices humans make that God will override? Here we get to the heart of the matter. One of, if not the, centrally important feature of God is divine goodness. Of course, we can't separate it from other features.

A good God without power would be ineffectual, for example. But what's attractive about theism is, arguably, that God is good. We don't want a God who both doesn't like us and who has a big stick with which to beat us. It is from God's goodness that value suffuses the world. When God makes humans in the divine image and places them into the world, God is placing people capable of love. We are capable of love because we have free will as a property. Without that property there would still be goodness in the world, but there would not be the kind of creative goodness—love—that comes with free will.

Freedom-as-capacity is logically prior to love. Indeed, it is logically prior to each and every choice we make. But if the world was meant to be a place of love and if that requires freedom-as-capacity, God must risk humans going wrong. Thus evil is in the world. But if the world was meant to be a place of love, and if that requires freedom-as-capacity, it doesn't follow that God has to allow every single choice a human makes. In particular, God doesn't have to allow a choice that would bring to an end the great value of freedom-as-capacity. Allowing a human to soul-suicide would be an end to the very possibility of goodness for that person. Neither would God bring about the end of the human person's soul for the same reason. To either allow or to cause the permanent cessation of a particular human's soul understood as having the property of robust freedom would be to undermine God's own nature as freely creative lover.

Here the point isn't that God is morally obligated to keep humans alive forever. Rather, the point is that not to do so is to challenge the structural nature of love that God built into the universe in the first place. God doesn't destroy human souls because God can't metaphysically do so. The metaphysics of the world is good, structured by love. To remove the thing that allows for love in a human is to disvalue the very structure of the world. To disvalue the very structure of the world is to disvalue God's creative freedom itself.

We might say, however, that God owns a human in the sense that we all own beauty. Goodness is a communal reality. For me to destroy a beautiful thing—even if I created it—is to destroy something that I don't truly own. I may have legal and even moral ownership. But love isn't about morality in the sense of obligations and duties, rules that must be followed. Love is about shared value. Love has come to see beyond one's local self-interest, the sort of self-interest that worries first about one's own status and value. Instead, one's sees the shared value of beauty, goodness, and truth. One doesn't cling to them, for they are not one's own.[7]

God doesn't cling to the divine freedom understood as something to be clung to individually. Rather, God clings to shared freedom—the freedom to engage and do the good, the beautiful, and the true. To end the freedom-as-capacity in any human, including those as yet unredeemed, would be to undermine the very structure of God's relationship to the world as valuable.

So God doesn't own humans, and the argument for the possibility of soul-cessation based on ownership fails. Of course, this alone doesn't show that humans aren't mortal. However, the argument from divine ownership fails in a way that at least points toward the fairly strong notion of immortality for humans. If humans have immortality, then we are not mortal and post-mortem annihilation is not possible. Not even God can destroy a being that is immortal (whether enduringly or essentially), once it exists. I'll return in the last chapter to explore an extended argument for immortality by picking up and explicating the pattern of reasoning found in this last section. First, however, let's consider whether humans can bring about their own soul-demise.

---

7. See Mavrodes, "Religion and the Queerness of Morality," for some interesting reflections on morality as a fallen version of love.

CHAPTER 4

Why Humans Can't Bring About Their Own Soul-Death

My main goal in this chapter is to explore whether humans can bring about their own soul-death.

Just as humans have no say over their creation, so they have no say over their permanent cessation. The creation and substance of a human person is due entirely to God. A human qua human can no more be the cause of its own end then it can be the cause of its own beginning. It seems entirely in the hands of God. Unlike with the cessation of an earthly human existence, the cessation of a human soul is permanent. The former is not really cessation, but only a change in venue. Perhaps one goes from this earthly mode of being to a more "stripped down" essential version of one's self. Or perhaps one ultimately is resurrected. But in either case, one does not truly cease to be. In the case of the permanent cessation of the human soul, however, there is no resurrection or continuation in another form. One's essence is permanently gone. We humans exist entirely within the causal, sustaining web of God's love. Hence while one might wish to cease to be, it's not more than a wish over something that is not in one's control. So it's not at all up to us to bring about our own, permanent cessation. Just as we have no power or influence over whether we are created in the first place, so it seems that we don't have the power or influence to cause our own (or anyone else's) permanent cessation. That's not the sort of beings we are. We are indeed contingent, but we cannot cease to be under our own power.

But perhaps God designed us to move from being something grand to being something less grand, from grumblers to mere grumbles as C. S. Lewis proposes the possibility.[1] If this continuum is possible, perhaps it runs all the way to nothingness. This seems to involve something like this. The sort of being we have is contingent, but becomes more or less real (that is, more or less interesting, mature, and so forth) depending on one's relationship with God. One's will might make sufficient moves away from a positive relationship with God in that one's being moves toward non-being in the Platonic sense Lewis seems to invoke. But notice that the woman in Lewis' story is still a grumble; there is something to her, just not much that is "substantial." This reflects two things. First, it points toward Plato's hierarchy of being from the Good through the forms, mathematics, physicality, and (mirror) images. So long as there is a "more real" being, perhaps there will be a "less real" being. Grumblers become mere grumbles. Things at the mirror end of reality are not non-existent; they are something closer to fakes. There can be a real rose picked fresh from the garden, a rose rearranged by human hands made from real rose petals (as one might imagine a float in the Rose Parade), and fake roses made of plastic and paper. Each of these is equally real in the sense that none of them are, say, fictional or "mere figments." But some are closer to natural or real, garden-picked roses. Some are more real than others, but all exist.[2] What's in Plato's mirror can only cease to be if the more real thing it copies ceases to be. But God cannot cease to be and hence neither can the reflections (the images) of the divine. Our being as sustained by God cannot cease to be on its own by human decision.

But note that while it may be the case that one cannot cause the permanent cessation of one's being, one may be able to cause a change in kind of being and hence cease to be as a human person. Changing oneself from being a grumbler to a grumble is an essential change from a person to a nonperson. One kind of thing becomes another. If by "soul" is meant "what is essential to a person," then actions that reduce one's degree of being could destroy the soul even though some being remains—if those actions removed what is essential to personhood. So there could be a reduction in being, and the person *qua person* could cease to be. Since that is what is at

---

1. See Lewis, *The Great Divorce*, 74–75.

2. This suggestion is due to Gregory Vlastos. See "Plato on Knowledge and Reality," 374–81.

stake, the argument that the cessation of the human person is not possible will need to be bolstered in other ways.[3]

How might we bolster the argument? As I noted in the first chapter, according to some understandings of the doctrine of hell and of self-determination, the unredeemed lack self-determination. Some suggest that they are wholly stripped of any kind of agency (they can't do anything anymore, even if they maintain sinful dispositions that would manifest as sinful actions were they able to act). Others hold a somewhat weaker view suggesting that because they are cut off from divine grace they are no longer free to act in any way other than in accord with sinful dispositions. That is, if the unredeemed have any free agency at all, it is of a wholly compatibilist character. If self-determination involves the ability to do otherwise than what one does—if it involves freedom in some more robust or libertarian sense—then the unredeemed no longer have self-determination according to traditional understandings of hell.[4] This seems implied in Lewis's grumbler becoming a grumble.

If we have robust self-determination, one might wonder if it is within one's power or ability to change oneself from a conscious being with robust self-determination to a conscious being with merely compatibilist sorts of freedoms. This question need not draw the same answer as the following one. Can one change oneself using robust self-determination from a person with robust self-determination to a being with no consciousness at all and hence no freedom to speak of? Perhaps the reason we think one can shoulder this latter task is that as we reflect on earthly suicide we suppose there is nothing beyond the earthly life.[5] If one commits suicide, then one has effectively changed oneself into the sort of being that is not conscious and not free. But this is quite a different answer than can be given to the first question. While it is obvious that one can end one's earthly existence as a self-determining being, it is far from obvious that one can change the nature of one's being as self-determining with robust free will into a being with some other kind of free will. And if robust self-determination is the

---

3. I owe this observation to a reviewer of an earlier version of this chapter.

4. The gist of this idea and that of the previous paragraph were noted in a reviewer's comments on an earlier version of this chapter.

5. One need not think that, of course. One might commit suicide in hopes that the afterlife is better than this one. My point is merely a logical one. If we do think earthly suicides causes permanent cessation, then of course we can by choice move from being one sort of being with robust freedom to another without any freedom at all. We do so by destroying ourselves entirely.

central property in virtue of which human value rests, then if one could "reduce" the sort of freedom one has from incompatibilist to mere compatibilist by willing it, one might very well will oneself out of being a human person and yet remain a functional "human" organism.[6]

My question is whether the C. S. Lewis-inspired suggestion that one might move down the ladder of being from one sort of thing to another (from a grumbler to a grumble) makes any sense if one assumes that it is brought about by one's own will. Can one metaphysically change oneself from being the sort of thing that has robust self-determination to the sort of thing that does not and thereby cease to be a human person? Here we need to take a closer look at the idea that one can change oneself from having a robust self-determining consciousness to something without consciousness at all. I suggested that earthly suicide—with the added proviso that the earthly life is all that is available to a human person—indicates that one can, in fact, change oneself using one's robust self-determination into a dead body without consciousness and hence without free will. I further suggested that this is different from the case of changing oneself from a being with robust self-determination to a being without that robust feature. But is it really different? It could be, but only if there is no life after death. Of course, the discussion of hell is premised on the claim that there is life after death. And if it is true that there is life after death, it may in fact be metaphysically impossible to cause one's essence to cease to be. Appealing to earthly suicide can't help us here, because for all we know either one's (dualistic or Thomistic) soul continues on with robust self-determination or one is resurrected in a new body with robust self-determination. So if it is not clear that one can reduce one's being from having robust self-determination to a being with "mere" compatibilist free will (or no free will at all), it is not clear that one can reduce one's being as robustly self-determinate to a being with no consciousness and hence no free will at all—given, of course, life after death in anything close to the traditional Christian account. So the Lewis-inspired suggestion above does not obviously work. If it doesn't work to reduce the sort of being one has to something lesser, it is certainly not obvious that one can reduce oneself to nothing at all simply by willing it.

This leaves us only with skepticism about whether humans can bring about their own permanent demise, not a successful argument that they can't. So we need some additional information. Suppose our reality depends

---

6. This is not as aptly stated as it could be. In fact, "one" doesn't change into another sort of being at all if one loses an essential property. One simply ceases to exist.

in significant ways on our relationship with God. Here I don't mean simply some sort of causal relationship, but rather a loving relationship. In the children's story by Margaret Williams, *The Velveteen Rabbit*, the toy rabbit becomes a real (flesh and blood) rabbit because it is loved so much by the ill child.[7] Arguably in the Christian tradition we are real—in fact, the whole of creation is real—not merely because God causes the created order, but because God *loves* it. It is worth reflecting a little on what this might mean. In the Christian scheme of things, the world is not merely "natural" but shot through with value. Being itself is valuable in the broadly Platonic tradition that has so shaped the church's theology. To be at all entails being loved and being loved entails being. Value, in short, cannot be separated from being. Here I do not simply mean that one has moral value, but that one has metaphysical value.

If we parallel the story of the velveteen rabbit to the Christian story, it should be noted that perhaps God's love alone is not enough to make us fully real (mature, interesting, etc.). For that we may need human response—the velveteen rabbit must love the child as well as be loved by the child. Since God's love doesn't change but our love does, our response to God shapes and molds us; in Platonic terms, it makes us "more real." A grumble is real, just not all that interesting, a grumbler more so, a grateful person more so, and a fully grateful person even more so. Is it possible that a human, by choice, causes her own cessation by moving away from loving God and hence toward being a grumble? That may be the case from our human point of view. But God, presumably, loves the grumble as much as God loves the fully developed and mature person. It would seem, then, that just as Plato's mirror image won't cease to be without the cessation of the Forms, neither will a human soul cease to be without the cessation of God's love. Although the mirror image is less mature or interesting—less real—than the thing it copies, its basic existence doesn't cease. In the case of humans, if we take self-determination as central to the soul, then the soul has little of interest to do and little "substantiality" when in the reduced, unloving state of hell. Hell may be excruciatingly boring, but it will not be empty. The soul is too important, too valuable, too loved by God to cease to be.

Now none of that answers the question of how we might "reduce" ourselves from conscious beings with robust self-determination to something less. God would have to permit such a change. But if God loves us, and by nature God is love, then God cannot let us. Indeed, not only can God not

---

7. Williams, *The Velveteen Rabbit*.

let us do so, not even God can reduce us in being. I'll say more of this in the next chapter.

For the moment, let's assume that souls cannot cease to be, so to speak, by their own hand. Nevertheless, what if the person in hell does not want to be there? One way of getting out of hell is the cessation of the soul, but that's ruled out. The other, of course, is to move from hell to heaven. Does God have the responsibility to take the unredeemed person out of hell when he doesn't wish to be there? Otherwise it seems that God would be infringing on his free will to choose not to be in hell.[8] Here it is arguable that the robust account of self-determination upon which the argument relies must leave open the possibility that people in hell can change their minds. It hence leaves open the possibility that one can discover that one doesn't want to be in hell after having arrived. But having arrived at that conclusion—given the overall Christian scheme of things and given enduring immortality—is tantamount to having arrived at the conclusion that one's happiness lies in the appropriate relationship with God.[9] While God might, on the view suggested here, be obligated to keep people in hell in existence because they are so valuable, it doesn't follow that the people in hell need to remain there. They can remain in existence in heaven just as well as they can in hell. If the very existence of a human person relies on being loved by God, God's love will forever sustain him with the hope that he will turn, finally, toward God.

But what if the person languishing in hell desires not merely not to be there but to cease to exist entirely? Does it make sense to say that God out of respect for self-determination must keep the person in existence? That, apparently, goes against actually valuing the person's grounded, concrete application of self-determination—freedom-as-choice. There is a tension here; God is respecting the continued existence of the capacity for self-determination—freedom-as-capacity—in a way that, at least arguably, fails to respect the creature's freedom-as-choice—the concrete effort to exercise such self-determination through self-annihilation. Now this problem may not be too serious if the creature lacks the metaphysical power to self-annihilate. The ball is entirely in God's court then. But the problem becomes more serious if the creature has this power and God simply denies the person's request to cease to be. I've already suggested that we humans don't

---

8. This point was raised by a reviewer of the earlier draft of the chapter.

9. Phil Smith commented here the following way: "Can a person in hell wish to not be in hell and not be lovingly related to God? Yes, in the sense that he could wish for round squares. Not even God can take you out of hell if hell is in you."

have that power, or at least that there is no clear reason to think we do. Yet it is not as strong an argument as we might wish. But if not even God can bring about the cessation of humans, then humans won't be able to either. To defend enduring immortality, we need a reason to think God doesn't have that power. This is the subject of the next chapter.

CHAPTER 5

An Argument for Immutable Immortality

Are humans immortal and if so, when do we gain that property? Annihilationists reject immortality simpliciter for humans, opting for conditional immortality for the redeemed. If we have immortality from natality forward, whether natural or immutable, we don't have conditional immortality and annihilationism fails as eschatologically in its claim to truth.

Section I lays out some details of this last claim. Section II presents the argument for immutable immortality.

I

As I noted in the previous chapter, in contemporary discussions of hell, some defend eternal conscious punishment and others annihilationism. Those who believe in eternal conscious punishment believe the unredeemed human person continues forever in a state of punishment. Annihilationists believe that the unredeemed human person simply ceases to be at some point, usually the final judgment or after some time in punishment. A key issue in this debate is whether immortality attends humans.

By saying humans are immortal it should now be clear that I mean to claim that humans exist forever, once created by God. Now humans might, as I suggested in chapter 2, have immortality as an essential property and as such immortality would true be of humans inherently, not something coming to us from the "outside" as an addition to one's being, but part and parcel of what it is to be a human. I call this "natural immortality." I will not argue for natural immortality. The reason is not too far to seek, for the idea that humans are essentially immortal requires that God could not have made humans without immortality, that is, that there is no possible world in which humans are mortal. I believe that is too strong a notion of immortality.

Instead, I argue for enduring immortality in the sense that immortality is a property such that once one has it, one cannot lose it. In fact, I argue that humans have strongly enduring immortality. Weakly enduring properties, one will recall, are properties that once one has them one cannot lose them so long as one exists. Strongly enduring properties are such that once one has them, there is no time one doesn't have them. Immortality, I suggest, is a property humans have in a strongly enduring manner. As it turns out, however, the argument also supports immortality as a weak immemorial property. So humans have immutable immortality.

Natural immortality contrasts with conditional immortality where humans are understood as created mortal but with the potential for immortality, an immortality not natural to us (essential to us) but granted (or not) at the final judgment. In either case—natural or conditional immortality—humans remain contingent. Humans are not necessary, but created beings. However, enduring immortality is compatible in principle with humans staring out as mortal and gaining immortality later. However, I will make the stronger claim that humans are created with the enduring property of immortality as part of God's plan for the created order. That plan includes granting humans free will as an essential property—a property in virtue of which humans can develop love—and humans having the essential property of free will implies that we have the enduring property of immortality from natality. So, there is no time when a given human person is mortal. Thus, I argue not only that humans have strongly enduringly immortality, but there is no time at all during the life of a human when she does not have that property. It is an immemorial property, although weakly so. God cannot, thus, simply let or cause a human to cease to be at the final judgment. Immortals cannot cease to be. They have immutable immortality.

Plato and other Hellenists held to an immortality that could be understood as inherent to humans. Indeed, they may have thought that humans are essentially or naturally immortal. In today's terms, Plato may even have thought humans were necessary beings, since they were like the forms. (I'll return to discuss this further in Appendix A.) He at least conceived of immortality as extending in both temporal directions; there never was a time when the soul did not exist. I will defend immortality as extending only into

An Argument for Immutable Immortality

the future, a view aligning closer with Christian accounts of creation where humans are created beings. There was a time, then, when any given human was not. Once created, however, humans by nature exist forever. Further, although humans may be essentially immortal, it seems more plausible to understand human immortality as an immutable property. I'll be satisfied, in short, with the more chastened claim about immortality.

Of course, the context for this entire discussion is the notion of eschatological annihilationism. Annihilationists often note that a theology of eternal conscious torture or punishment is rooted in an extra-biblical, Hellenistic (perhaps Platonic) doctrine of immortality. Consider Clark Pinnock writing to defend annihilationism: "I am convinced that the Hellenistic belief in the immortality of the soul has done more than anything else (specifically more than the Bible) to give credibility to the doctrine of everlasting conscious punishment of the wicked. This belief, not Holy Scripture, is what gives this doctrine the credibility it does not deserve."[1] In short, the cultural baggage the ancients brought to Scripture led them to read it as teaching that unredeemed souls will continue to exist postmortem because they are by nature immortal and must dwell somewhere, hell being the obvious choice.[2]

---

1. Pinnock, "The Destruction of the Finally Impenitent," in Date, Stump, and Anderson, eds., *Rethinking Hell*, 67. For similar comments, see Travis, "The Nature of Final Destiny" in the same volume. For other comments linking Hellenism to the doctrine of eternal conscious punishment, see Brandyberry, "Important Forgotten History" in *A Consuming Passion*, 247. It's worth noting that Brandyberry does not make the strong claim that immortality is behind eternal conscious punishment, but rather that Hellenism was influential in the ancient thinking about hell. One could suggest that the early thinkers considered Scripture, derived eternal conscious punishment and hence concluded that the soul was immortal rather than assuming immortality and thus finding eternal conscious punishment in Scripture. For other discussions of conditional immortality and annihilationism, see Hughes, "Is the Soul Immortal"; Marshall, "Divine and Human Punishment in the New Testament"; Wright, "A Kinder, Gentler Damnation?"; and Swinburne, "The Future of the Totally Corrupt," all in *Rethinking Hell*.

2. The annihilation of the unredeemed is possible only if the human soul is not *by nature* eternal. The unredeemed can thus cease to be while the redeemed gain conditional immortality—immortality sustained forever by God. Sometimes the terms *annihilationism* and *conditional immortality* are used interchangeably. This is mistaken, as noted by theologian Clark Pinnock, who is quoted above. Although the latter is necessary for the former, annihilationism is not required by conditional immortality. But Pinnock's claim, although a good corrective, is not strictly accurate either. Humans could be naturally mortal without also having the possibility of conditional immortality. Mortality is what is required for the possible annihilation of the human person. Arguably even after the final judgment, the heaven-bound are mortal by nature. God simply sustains the human

But what if souls do have created but natural immortality and we have good reason to think they do? Affirmative answers could change the

---

soul forever. It is strictly God's creative and constant activity that generates a non-natural immortality for the redeemed. This non-natural immortality could be a version of what I've called "enduring immortality," but not one granted humans on earth. But is the soul enduringly or naturally immortal? Besides exegesis of New Testament passages, theologians and philosophers propose various arguments to defend one or the other of two groups of views. The first group contains the ideas of ECT for the unredeemed, heaven for the redeemed, and the typically affiliated natural immortality supporting both. The second group is annihilationism with its affiliated natural mortality and life in heaven with its conditional immortality. Let me illustrate. Stephen Travis writes: "The case for eternal punishment [ECT] rests primarily on belief in the immortality of the soul, the requirement of divine justice that the sins of this life should be appropriately punished in the next, and the apparently explicit teaching of biblical passages such as Matt 25:34, 41, 46; Mark 9:42f; 2 Thess 1:9; Rev 14:11; 19:3; 20:10." In contrast, the case for conditional immortality and annihilation includes: *First*, the claim that immortality of the soul is a non-biblical doctrine derived from Greek philosophy. In biblical teaching man [sic] is "conditionally immortal"—that is, he has the possibility of becoming immortal as a gift from God. *Second*, biblical images such as "fire" and "destruction" suggest annihilation rather than continuing existence. *Third*, New Testament references to "eternal punishment" do not automatically mean what they have traditionally been assumed to mean. "Eternal" may signify the permanence of the *result* of judgment, rather than the continuation of the act of punishment itself. *Fourth*, we must recognize that such New Testament language is picture-language. The fact that Jesus can speak of hell in terms of both "darkness" and "fire" surely makes it clear that such language must not be taken too literally. *Fifth*, eternal torment serves no useful purpose, and therefore exhibits a vindictiveness incompatible with the love of God. *Finally*, eternal punishment requires that we believe in heaven and hell existing forever "alongside" each other. It seems impossible to reconcile this with the conviction that God will be "all in all" (1 Cor 15:28). And James Brandyberry quotes six different authors noting the influence of Greek thought on the Christian doctrine of immortality. My main concern is to focus on a point made by Travis and Pinnock, viz., that ECT rests on the natural immortality of the soul from Greek philosophy. The argument seems to be this: It is popularly held that the Hellenistic view of the soul as immortal is true. If that view is true, then God has to do *something* with the immortal-but-recalcitrant souls at the judgment. Since the souls can't be destroyed and they can't live in heaven with God, they must be sent to hell, which will itself last forever because the souls there are immortal. It's interesting, however, that in the six quotations found in Brandyberry, all describing the historical development of ECT, none makes the stronger claim made by Travis and Pinnock. They simply make the general point that Greek thought influenced accounts of the afterlife. No surprise there. Being an influence, however, is not the same as being the *grounding* source. It could be that people found ECT taught in Scripture and concluded that the Greeks were right. If, in fact, Scripture teaches that in the afterlife one either goes to live forever with God or forever with the devil, then it follows that humans are, indeed, immortal. So the immortality of the soul may be a metaphysical conclusion drawn from theological and exegetical work on Scripture, rather than the reverse. See Fudge, *The Fire that Consumes*; Date, Stump, and Anderson, eds., *Rethinking Hell*; and Date and Highfield, eds., *A Consuming Passion*.

landscape of the recent debate over hell. I think this is especially true if the argument derives not from an extra-biblical source but from the broad teaching of the Christian Scriptures. Of course, I don't argue for natural immortality here. I do, however, argue for enduring immortality and that that immortality is something with which we are created. Thus, although something short of natural immortality, immutable immortality is enough to undermine conditional immortality.

Although I've begun the discussion by reference to those who defend eternal-conscious-punishment notions of hell, nothing in the argument below entails eternal conscious punishment. Universalism might well be true. What's ruled out, on the success of the argument, is annihilationism. To lay my cards on the table, however, I have sympathy for annihilationism. I much prefer it over the idea that God has an eternal punishment in store for the unrepentant. Nevertheless, I suspect that annihilationists, in their enthusiasm for their project of rejecting both eternal conscious punishment and universalism, have been too quick in their rejection of natural immortality (or what will function in a similar manner, immutable immortality). Further, I suspect that part of the motivation (for many annihilationists) in rejecting Hellenistic immortality is just that it is, in fact, extra-biblical. It is not a rejection of the position per se, but its extra-biblical source. My goal thus is to provide a philosophical argument rooted in Christian theology, which in turn is itself rooted in Scripture. Such an argument will bring pressure on the biblical annihilationist's position. To reach that goal, the argument below stands free of support found in biblical passages dealing with the eschaton. Instead it provides a replacement for the traditional Hellenistic views that souls are immortal, a view that perhaps shaped the reading of the eschatological biblical passages. As to whether Scripture is itself committed to eternal conscious punishment for the unredeemed I will pass over in silence, it being no part of my goal to defend that logically separate view.

Let's say that some humans decide to use their freedom-as-capacity to choose for soul cessation (freedom-as-choice). If God not only allows but encourages the use of free will, one might think that God must honor this particular freedom-as-choice. But that is less than clear for there may be exceptions to what is apparently God's general hands-off policy toward human choices. In other words, there may be limits to what God can allow in terms of freedom-as-choice. Here some further care is needed.

In one sense, God can overrule human freedom-as-choice, for surely God can—in divine providence—overrule the results of human free choices for some greater good. For example, suppose Jones attempts to push Smith over a cliff in order to kill Smith. Suppose, further, that he succeeds in the act of pushing Smith over the cliff. Now God, having other plans for Smith, arranges it so that Smith is caught in a tree growing just over the edge of the cliff and is thereby saved. Jones's intention to kill Smith—his freedom-as-choice to do so—is thus thwarted by God. Indeed, this sort of thing may happen all the time and humans be unaware that the thwarting of their goals is brought about by God. But note that God intervenes in cases such as this after the human freedom-as-choice is made. God doesn't stop Jones from making the choice and following through. God simply fixes the results differently than Jones had hoped. So God's general hands-off policy seems to apply mostly to the human act of choosing. God may intervene after the fact to bring about different ends than a given human wished. So when I say that God has a general hands-off policy, I mean that usually, so far as we can tell, God gives us freedom-as-capacity and lets us use it to make whatever freedom-as-choice we make.

Are there exceptions to this general rule? There might be. Consider the case of Jones and Smith again. But suppose this time, God interferes with Jones's choice by causing him to die of a heart attack just before pushing Smith to his death. Here God still allows Jones to make the choice. The only difference between the old and new description is that God intervenes earlier. God doesn't stop the choice from being made. Might God sometimes, in divine foreknowledge of what Jones would decide and given certain circumstances, cause Jones to die before making the choice? Perhaps. But that, somehow, seems to cheapen our view of God and the gift of free will. If God could do such things, why did the divinity fail to intervene before Adam chose to eat the fruit? Had God intervened, not only would sin have not entered the world but the very notion that we have freedom-as-capacity would be undermined. It may be that any intervention God does in the human ordering of things (as rooted in our free will) comes after the choice is made and never before. For God to intervene in freedom-as-choice before the choice is made is simply for God to not allow for human free will at all.

God's hands-off policy seems rooted in the very nature of the created order itself. This becomes clearer when discussing immortality. In the case of humans deciding to permanently end their being (as opposed to the temporary cessation of Smith as he hits bottom only to appear in the afterlife), the choice entails the end forever of their freedom-as-capacity. In the Smith and Jones case, it may be that God doesn't allow Jones to make a choice at all but that that disability is short-lived. Perhaps instead of causing Jones to die of a heart attack, God causes a brain glitch that disallows free-will choices just for the moment. Later, Jones is free to make choices again. The really telling case occurs when a choice has permanent results.

Under these conditions of permanence, it seems that God is in a bind. On the one hand, God's moral policy seems to be to let people do what they choose (to the extent that all humanity falls into sin, in fact). But God's policy—moral respect for each concrete free choice—is logically dependent on the fact that the freedom-as-capacity is inherently valuable—metaphysically valuable, we might say—for it is the metaphysical ground of any freedom-as-choice. So in this one case—the case of humans choosing to end their souls forever—if God follows the moral policy of a "hands-off" approach, God has to respect not merely a bad choice but a *very* bad choice, a choice so bad it undermines the very capacity for choice. Free will—which could very well be the metaphysical motivation for all of the created order, a good so great that God lets humanity cause the fall of that order—would undermine God's overall goal for the universe, viz., to make a universe full of freely loving human persons.

It is generally recognized that freedom-as-capacity does not imply freedom to in fact accomplish whatever ends we might imagine. In each of the following cases, one might be able to do the mental feat of willing, but not the factual feat of making changes in the world. There are logical limits (we are not free to be and not be at the same time and the same way), nomological limits (we are not free to fly beyond the speed of light), and moral-metaphysical limits (we are not free to turn treachery into a good). Just so, there may be self-referential limits to free will. No human is free to eliminate one's freedom-as-capacity by one's freedom-as-choice. One may be free to will one's own permanent cessation (let's say, to form the intention to end one's permanent cessation), but the ability to actually end one's freedom-as-capacity won't follow from the freedom-as-choice.[3] Just as Jones wills to kill Smith by casting him off the cliff but is thwarted in doing so by God's convenient arrangement of a cliff-hanging tree, so God allows humans to choose to end it all, permanently, but thwarts their practical ability to do so. Here, however, God does not thwart the human freedom-as-choice for some greater good (for Smith, let's say, or any other specific

---

3. I thank Phil Smith for suggesting the parallel sorts of limitations.

historical situation), but rather because to allow the cessation of the human soul undermines the structural goodness of the created order itself and, indeed, undermines God's own goodness itself, goodness understood as love.

The self-referential limit is not clearly a logical or nomological limit. It seems closer to a moral-metaphysical limit. But it isn't merely that one ought not to will one's permanent demise. There is nothing in a moral prohibition that keeps us from willing and accomplishing immoral actions. The self-referential limit seems more like the moral-metaphysical example provided above—one can't successfully will treachery to be good. Now one might choose to do so. One might choose to turn treachery into good. But one can't, in metaphysical fact, do so. Likewise in the self-referential case. One can't (successfully) will the permanent cessation of the willing capacity itself. To do so would be turning a metaphysically good thing (freedom-as-capacity) into a metaphysically bad thing (the lack of freedom-as-capacity). The limit here, however, seems not so much a moral limit (one would act morally badly if one turned treachery into a good) as a moral-metaphysical limit, a metaphysical limit about the nature of morality. One can't turn what is bad by nature—treachery—into what is good by nature. Neither can one turn what is good by nature—the capacity for freedom—into a bad thing—the lack of capacity. Of course, when one turns something into nothing at all, it's not entirely perspicuous whether one has made a bad thing. Rather, one has simply removed something from reality. Nothingness is, one may think, neither bad nor good. But in the Platonic/Augustinian/Christian tradition, being is fundamentally good and moving from being to non-being is bad—metaphysically bad.

But why think that? I'll explore that question below. Whether there is a metaphysical, self-referential limit on freedom-as-capacity of the sort outlined turns on linking being and goodness. If there is such a limit, some metaphysical grounds need to be provided for thinking so. In doing so, we will also have a partial answer, at least, to why moving from being to non-being is metaphysically bad. The argument below will do just that, if it is successful.

II

I do not believe human immorality is a necessary or essential feature of humans. That is, it seems to me that God creates humans with a certain sort of value and from that value it follows that God cannot, without undermining

An Argument for Immutable Immortality

the divine nature, destroy or allow to be destroyed, the value God has created. I think, instead of immortality being an essential property, it is a immutable property. There is no time at which a being with an immutable property can cease to have it. Having a strongly enduring property is consistent with also being a contingent being.

The argument I provide relies on some basic truths held by Christian (and other) theists. Nevertheless, the argument is philosophical in nature and does not rely on scriptural authority except insofar as Christian theism itself derives from Scripture. The argument makes no direct appeal to biblical references dealing with post-life matters and falls prey to none of the foibles of scriptural hermeneutics. Indeed, one of the argument's strengths is that its conclusion can be used as a broad hermeneutical framework for reading relevant eschatological passages. If the argument is sound, a Christian eschaton in which the unredeemed are annihilated is not tenable. So I turn to provide an argument for the claim that God cannot bring about the total destruction of a human person. Hence, humans are strongly immutably immortal. This chapter, in short, fleshes out the details of the argument for immortality briefly suggested in chapter 3.

We are now in a position to present and explore a metaphysical argument for immutable immortality. I'll refer to the central argument as the master argument. Other supporting arguments follow below.

Master Argument:

1. All other things being equal, if an event interferes with a human h's freedom, the event is metaphysically bad. (Premise)
2. An event leading to the permanent cessation of human h is an event that interferes with h's freedom. (Premise)
3. Therefore, an event leading to the permanent cessation of a human h is metaphysically bad. (1, 2)
4. Some metaphysically bad events would undermine the divine nature were they to occur. (Premise)
5. It is impossible for events to occur that would undermine the divine nature. (Premise)
6. The permanent cessation of a human is a metaphysically bad event that undermines the divine nature. (Premise)
7. Therefore, the permanent cessation of a human is impossible. (3, 4, 5, 6)

8. If the permanent cessation of the human is impossible, humans are immutably immortal. (Premise)

9. Therefore, humans are immutably immortal. (7, 8)

The key is 6 and it needs separate support. I'll call that support the Cessation Argument. The Cessation Argument relies on a number of others, each of which builds on an earlier one. I'll present these below.

First, however, a comment about 1 and 2. "Freedom," as I've noted, is ambiguous between freedom-as-capacity and freedom-as-choice. The latter relies on the former. Which sense do 1 and 2 use? Well, one cannot choose permanent cessation without choosing to have one's freedom-as-capacity ended. But one cannot choose such an eventuality without using one's capacity to choose it. Premise 1, then is neutral between capacity and choice. Premise 2, however, must refer to capacity because it is only with the cessation of one's freedom-as-capacity that one's being ceases to continue.

The idea that self-determination undergirds metaphysical goodness needs some exploration. I propose that whatever else is essential to the human person, self-determination and the concomitant free will are the central features of being a human person and, indeed, the very individual human person one is. According to Christian theology, humans are made in the image of God. As such, humans have at least some features God has. I want to explore freedom through this theological concept, however briefly.

What features does God have? God is powerful, creative, knowledgeable, emotional, social, and good. The Christian commitment to these features can easily be drawn from Scripture. A deeper question arises when we ask whether God is free. The Scriptures speak little of God's freedom. But perhaps it is everywhere assumed and is therefore better understood as an inference from (some of) these other features.

The attribution to God of freedom is sometimes thought philosophically problematic. The problems with God's freedom usually begin with the observation that God is good but that God's goodness is different from human goodness. We humans can fail to do good (in our freedom), but God, it would seem, cannot. So perhaps to show that God is free we should begin somewhere other than with God's goodness, at least if we understand God's goodness primarily through the notion of moral rules and principles that must be followed by an entirely good being.

If we begin with God's creativity, we don't obviously run into the same set of problems as we do when we think of morality. Moral goodness with its rules and principles seems, somehow, fixed. God, in order to be morally good, has a straight and narrow path to follow. Being morally good, in other words, is strictly circumscribed. One doesn't make morality up as one goes along, but rather it is uncovered as we uncover the nature of things. But creativity is different. Indeed, creativity by its nature is not circumscribed. Or at least not so narrowly circumscribed. Creativity for God seems as open as the divine can think up (broadly logical) possibilities. So from God's creativity it seems safe to infer God's freedom.

So if we are made in God's image, we are made free. What type of freedom? Since freedom is linked to creativity, and God's creativity is, according to the tradition, *ex nihilo* creativity, one might suggest that human freedom is likewise linked to the possibility of bringing something into being from nothing. What do we bring into existence from nothing? Our choices and the actions that follow from them. We are most like God when we act freely in the robust sense on which this argument rests. Does that entail that robust self-determination is the main feature of humans in virtue of which they are what they are or in virtue of which they are valuable? Perhaps not, at least all by itself. But our freedom is fundamental, not only to our creativity, but to our (moral) goodness, to our social lives, to our use (or abuse) of power. Without freedom, these other features pale in significance to what they are with freedom. So I think one can safely claim that our robust self-determinative capacity is the central feature of being human and being valuable.

If indeed, self-determination and its concomitant free will are valuable features of the world, they are valuable because the world itself is "shot through" with value. The world is fundamentally, on the Christian scheme of things, normative and that normativity relies on a robust notion of free will. Now free will aligned with evil cheapens the world, makes it less than God intended. Free will aligned with the good, however, makes the world better. Perhaps God cannot cause or allow the destruction of the human soul because to do so is logically connected to God's causing or allowing the destruction of the possibility of goodness coming to fruition in the world. God doesn't avoid the cessation of the human soul merely because of a tangential feature of God's existence. God cannot wipe humans out because of the objective value of freedom, a freedom that finds its roots in God's being.[4] In that way, perhaps, Plato was right. Humans are like the forms, at least the form of robust self-determination. And that, in itself, is a metaphysical good.

But when we think of God's properties, we perhaps impose some of our own limitations. God's freedom is a case in point. We worry whether God can be free when we think of God's being morally good and the possibility—if God is really free—of choosing immorally. Doesn't God's essential moral goodness rule out the divine freely choosing? But if we think of morality as a fallen version of love[5]—a set of rules and regulations to keep humans from killing and hurting each other—then perhaps morality doesn't apply to God at all. Rather what applies to God is the "rule" of love. Love is much more creative and open than morality. God's having the property of free will provides the ground for thinking free will in humans is valuable. In God, however, no concrete free choice is ever evil, but always good. Thus, although one can separate in discussion God's having the property of free will and God's actual concrete choices flowing from that free will, in concrete fact one cannot separate the value of God's freedom from the free actions the divine does.

Unfortunately, with humans one can separate the value of the freedom itself from the things we do with that freedom. The human use of the capacity for free choices does not always line up with the goodness of the universe God created, or at least the universe God wants to bring about. But God knows that in our human freedom-as-capacity we can choose better.

---

4. Perhaps, as Robin Parry, Wipf and Stock's indefatigably insightful editor, suggested to me, this is an argument against God annihilating *all* humans, but need it be an argument against his annihilating *any* humans? Humans with free will may be essential to God's purposes, but is any specific human essential in the same way? After all, God's purposes could be fulfilled if my parents had not freely chosen to have sex and thereby conceive me. So I—and my freedom—are not essential to God's cosmic purpose. Thus, even if the annihilation of free will is a problem, is my annihilation a problem? My response to Robin is this: While perhaps losing one or two or even a great number of humans won't undermine God's purposes, I think the focus of the criticism is in the wrong place. According to Robin's observation, God's purposes would avoid being thwarted only if at least some people are redeemed. But what if no one is and God annihilates everyone as damned? Surely God's purposes would be undermined. Here what is important is the objective value of free will, a value rooted in what we are (and what God is) and not in what we do with the free will. To wipe out free will, even if used badly, undermines the whole project.

5. See Mavrodes, "Religion and the Queerness of Morality," 213–26.

An Argument for Immutable Immortality

Perhaps so long as that hope remains, God cannot destroy the human capacity for freedom. Freedom's capacity for goodness is rooted in the very nature of God and God will hold out, and indeed, must hold out, for a better result. That is God's nature, and it follows from the fact that humans are not yet perfected that God will—indeed must—always side with hope. God does so of a divine freedom that is not open to evil, but only to love, creative in all its possibilities. Thus, instantiations of free will—human souls—cannot be destroyed without undermining the very concrete nature of God's hopes for the future and, indeed, God's very nature itself and the purposes for which God created the world—to instantiate more divine love. God cannot destroy human souls because to do so is to undermine the deeply normative and valuable structure of the universe and thereby undermine God's own metaphysical value. But how might the argument for that conclusion go? That is the burden of the remainder of this essay.

Premise 4 also needs a brief comment. For an event to undermine God's nature, the event would have to be inconsistent with God's nature. So, just as God cannot perform the logically impossible, neither can God allow, or cause, an event that undermines God's nature. Such a state of affairs would be inconsistent.

I turn now to defend 6. As noted above, I call the supporting argument the Cessation argument. It is supported by a number of other arguments, the first of which is the Love-ladeness argument:

Love-ladeness Argument

A. All God's acts are acts from the divine nature. (Premise)
B. All acts done from the divine nature and everything that results from such acts are laden with love. (Premise)
C. God's *ex nihilo* creation of the world is an act God does. (Premise)
D. Therefore, God's *ex nihilo* creation of the world and the created order that results from it are laden with love. (A, B, C)

A creative action and its products are laden with love. The phrase "laden with love" captures the deeply rooted sense found in theism that because God is good, the created order is shot through with value. Theism, as opposed to a hard-core naturalism, need not invent value (moral, aesthetic, or otherwise) because the world itself is metaphysically valuable. That value is, ultimately, derived from God and the divine creative activity. The created order is laden with love.

Next, the Metaphysical Goodness Argument:

E. Anything laden with love is metaphysically good. (Premise)

F. Therefore, to be (an extra-divine entity) is to be metaphysically good. (D, E)

G. Therefore, humans are metaphysically good. (F)

This argument simply specifies what is meant by "metaphysical good."
Onto the Love and Freedom Argument:

H. Some types of metaphysical goodness involve not only love-ladeness, but also the capacity to love and hence to make more love-ladeness.

I. God made humans in the divine image. (Premise)

J. Anything made in God's image is capable of love and hence making more love-ladeness. (Premise)

K. Therefore, the human type of metaphysical goodness is a type capable of love and hence making more love-ladeness. (H, I, J)

L. To be capable of love and making love-ladeness entails freedom-as-capacity. (Premise)

M. Therefore, humans have freedom-as-capacity. (J, K)

Our capacity for love, as a central aspect of the image of God in us, allows us not only to love but to create things that are laden with love. The capacity for love is built on a foundation of freedom-as-capacity. That is, in fact, the nature of freedom-of-capacity when it is aligned with goodness. Using free will to do evil cheapens or lessens the value of the world.

Goal Argument:

N. God's goal in creating the world is to create extra-divine metaphysical goodness. (Premise)

O. Therefore, God's goal in creating the world is to create more love-ladeness. (N, E)

God is love and out of the divine love God creates the world. Although no explicit reason is given in the Christian Scriptures as to why God created the world, love is often cited as the reason.[6] God's love is given to the

---

6. It may be that some Reformed folk will want to get off the argumentative bus here, for in some Reformed theology, God doesn't love everyone. It is no coincidence, perhaps, that it is those same folk who think eternal conscious punishment in hell is fair. I'll not

An Argument for Immutable Immortality

world in its creation and given that humans are made in the divine image and have the power to create, it is not implausible to think that God not only created the world with extra-divine metaphysical goodness, but made humans to continue to create more extra-divine goodness.

Replete with Goodness Argument

> P. Humans are always capable of creating more love-ladeness, that is, humans are always capable of making the world more replete with metaphysical goodness. (E, K, M)

The power of human creative love mirrors that of God. Our creative propensities, if not our actual creative work, are open to the future, open to change, open to more and more goodness.

God's Nature Argument

> Q. God's goals cannot be separated from God's nature. (Premise)
>
> R. Therefore, anything God does that undermines God's goals undermines God's nature. (Q)

God acts from God's nature. Since God is good, God cannot act in any other way but from goodness. Goodness here, as discussed earlier, is not mere morality, but pure, creative love. Such love desires only what is good. God's goals, then, can only be for good.

Permanent Cessation Argument

> S. The permanent cessation of the human person removes the freedom-as-capacity. (Premise)
>
> T. The removal of freedom-as-capacity removes the capability to love. (Premise)
>
> U. Therefore, the permanent cessation of a human person makes it impossible for that given human to make the world more replete with metaphysical goodness. (S, T)

A human choice to end one's soul is a choice to destroy freedom-as-capacity. Here we see why, no matter how much a human person might wish, hope, and choose to come to a permanent end, that human cannot bring it about on their own. Furthermore, by the removal of the capacity for freedom, one's ability to love ceases entirely. The cessation of the capability to

---

enter that discussion further here.

love simply removes the possibility of making anything with metaphysical goodness.

Finally, we reach the Cessation Argument

- V. To remove the possibility of a human making the world more replete with metaphysical goodness undermines God's plan. (Premise)
- W. Hence, allowing or causing the cessation of human free will undermines God's nature. (U., V.)
- X. The capacity for love and hence freedom-as-capacity are essential properties of humans. (Premise)
- Y. Therefore, the permanent cessation of a human is a metaphysically bad event that undermines the divine nature. (W., X.)

Y is identical to 6.

The instantiation of free will as a capacity is essential to the human person. It is, in short, part of the human soul without which nothing can be human. Yet it doesn't follow from that fact that God must morally abide by every freedom-as-choice made by humans, especially those that undermine freedom-as-capacity. Yet the following principle also seems to be true:

Self-Determination Principle (SDP): All other things being equal, an event is metaphysically bad whenever it leads to the undermining of freedom-as-capacity.

Is this principle true?

Those who defend eternal conscious punishment sometimes argue that God must respect the free will of human individuals. This respect eventuates in the notion that if a human person decides, ultimately—presumably in some fully knowledgeable and fully rational context—to reject God's love, that person will live forever in hell. Merely respecting the actual choices of humans, however, is not a strong enough basis for the notion that God cannot bring about or allow the cessation of the human soul, for God's having to respect human free will is a two-edged sword. If God has to respect human freedom-as-choice and a human freely chooses annihilation, won't God have to follow through? It appears that the defender of (natural) immortality will have to say something stronger than merely that God is morally bound to keep such souls alive forever.

To take steps toward a metaphysical claim that God cannot destroy humans who have free will, we need to repeat an observation made above. In general, God not only lets people use their free will to make choices of a wide variety, but the making of those choices is, in fact, the main point of creation (with the proviso that those choices ultimately lead to a good world). God's goal is to make free creatures who shape and mold the world. We know this, arguably, because God even lets moral evil and sin enter the world by free choice. It would seem, from this, that the divine attitude toward free-will choices is that they are of perhaps the greatest value. This is all reflected in free-will defenses against the problem of evil.

But such an appeal is not enough. We need to shift from morality to love. As a beginning step, instead of focusing on obligations to respect the person's choice, let's think of metaphysical value. Free will can be valued simply as the sort of thing it is—freedom-as-capacity. Its nature as a value-making property is such that if one has the property, one is more valuable than one would be without it. But free will can be valued in its concrete applications—freedom-as-choice. Here it is in virtue of the actual choices one makes using that feature that one is valuable. When this contrast is brought out, one may find oneself confused as to whether freedom-as-capacity takes priority over freedom-as-choice or the reverse in terms of metaphysical value. Having the capacity for self-determination leaves open the possibility that one makes either good choices or bad ones. When we are talking about which value is greater it may be hard to separate freedom-as-capacity from freedom-as-choice. But since God is a loving God who desires that no one perish, it seems that God would see freedom-as-capacity value as greater than freedom-as-choice value when at the point of concrete choice the agent chooses so poorly that that person undermines freedom understood either way. God may thus override the concrete choice because God wants the individual to have more time to choose better and wants, thereby, to retain the freedom-as-capacity value.

Another way to put this point is that the ultimate or full value of having robust free will is found only when one chooses the good. God, being the good itself, desires not only that we have the capacity to choose freely and to make our own characters, but God desires that we construct ourselves well—to make our characters truly worthwhile. The universe has an increase in value, in other words, when we use the metaphysically valuable freedom-as-capacity we have to make the universe a better place than when we use it to make the universe worse. God is always seeking, so to speak, more goodness, more love. God's granting the unregenerate's desire to cease to be cuts off the possibility of an increase in goodness and love to which we humans were designed to contribute. The value of a universe with the continued capacity for good choices is worth overriding the value of a negative or bad application of robust self-determination. God can respect the capacity of freedom—freedom-as-capacity—so much that God disvalues a bad choice made using the capacity. This disvaluing is no mere arbitrary choice on God's part. Rather, given the centrality of love to the very fabric of the universe, God cannot do otherwise.

Is it acceptable to continue to keep a person's soul alive forever when it desires its own permanent end? The answer is more complicated then it first seems. On the level of how God views the metaphysical value of having freedom, God cannot destroy any freedom-as-capacity without undermining the entire web of created existence and also the divine nature itself. God causes the world to be because of divine love. At the ontological core of what it means to love is a will utterly set toward love and the creative ways of expanding it. If one must speak of obligation, any obligation God has is ultimately to provide further opportunities to love. So while God cannot destroy freedom-as-capacity—a particular instantiation of free will in a given human—neither would God have an obligation to do so. Just, in fact, the opposite. That is, if the term "obligation" is the right term at all.

Let's return to the notion that human free will has various sorts of limits. Perhaps we cannot use freedom-as-capacity to limit freedom-as-capacity. This limitation is not logical or nomological, but moral-metaphysical. Is God bound by the same metaphysical truth? God, of course, cannot use the divine freedom-as-capacity to limit itself in terms of goodness. God is a necessary being and God's properties are essential to God. Now while freedom-as-capacity is essential to humans qua humans, we are not necessary beings. So if there is a self-referential limitation on human free will, it must be rooted in something other than necessity since humans are not necessary beings. But we may be immutably immortal. If we were immutably immortal, and radical self-determination were essential to us, we would not be able to bring about our end by choosing to bring it about. But of course, one can hardly appeal to immortality to show that one has immortality. So one might ask what reason there is to think that self-referential limitation exists for humans. I've argued that there is no clear reason to think that humans can reduce their status from people with robust free will to something less. We now have a reason that explains why we have no clear reason. Human freedom-as-capacity is a central part of the warp and woof of the good universe God created and to undo human freedom-as-capacity

An Argument for Immutable Immortality

would be for God to undo the divine goal and purpose for the created order and thereby to undo God's own nature.

In the case of self-referential limitation, one cannot use one's own freedom-as-capacity to limit one's freedom-as-capacity. But can God limit a human's freedom-as-capacity? If my intuition is correct, no. For God to cause or allow the destruction of the very thing that makes concrete goodness possible in the created order would be for God to allow or cause the divine goodness to be impossible. God is good metaphysically because God is love, which requires freedom-as-capacity. For God to undermine human freedom-as-capacity is tantamount to God undermining divine freedom-as-capacity. Here we might suggest that sometimes interference with self-determination is justified among humans because of the maturity level of the person involved—a parent stopping a young child from running across the street, perhaps. We can and should force that young child not to cross the street, because she isn't mature enough yet to know the danger. So perhaps God is waiting for the immature-because-unrepentant human person to see the better path. I won't pursue this theme further here.

But that brings me to an incidental and yet important point in regard to the argument for immutable immortality. Some who write of eternal conscious punishment speak of an "ultimate choice" humans make, for or against God. For some, the so-called "ultimate choice" that condemns one to a hell of eternal conscious punishment seems unconscionable. There are, of course, arguments against it I cannot rehearse here. But if the argument of this chapter is correct, it is not so much unconscionable as it is impossible. Free will is structured as open to the future and is rooted in God's nature and futurity itself. If that sort of freedom is essential to being human and it is as humans that those in hell must suffer (otherwise, hell seems fundamentally unfair, for those being punished are not, in fact, those who did the crime, but some lesser sort of being) then it is always possible to choose better. So hell could exist as a place for those to dwell while thinking over their sins, but it is closer to some pictures of purgatory as a sort of basement of heaven where one can ultimately only go up or sit on the same step until one is willing to move up. One cannot descend the steps. Perhaps Thomas Talbott is right. Ultimately God will—indeed, must—remove all limitations in humans so they can see that the only rational choice is to move toward God. Under those circumstances, everyone will move toward God.[7] So eternal conscious punishment need not result from immutable

---

7. Talbott, *Inescapable Love*.

immortality and hell will eventually be emptied. Can those in heaven choose to move back toward hell or a sinful life? I do not know. But the following might guide our thoughts. Even though one cannot choose freely to destroy one's soul, one can perhaps choose freely to become more like God. As one does so, one changes so that love is fundamental to one's nature and one's freedom is open to creatively putting love into action. One would never, as a fully loving person, choose harm over goodness, any more than would God. While we remain free in heaven, we no longer can choose evil. Indeed, that may very well have been God's goal from the beginning, to bring us always further into the light.

Appendix A

Some Speculative Metaphysical Structure

The argument for immortality given here stands free of biblical exegesis and although it makes plenty of metaphysical points, it does not develop a broader way of thinking about the status of properties vis-à-vis God and how that may be related to immortality. While this appendix has little by way of argument and lots by way of suggestion, its purpose is not necessarily to convince but to prompt further thinking about immortality and its relationship to what philosophers call the necessities—propositions, numbers, and properties (to name a few).

I will use some reflections on Plato's argument for the immortality of soul as a starting place to reflect about what might be needed, metaphysically, to understand human immortality. I've already noted my hesitancy about claiming that immortality is an essential property of humans, and my intuition that it is an immutable property. Indeed, had Plato had the conceptual tools of contemporary philosophy, perhaps he would have suggested exactly that.

The context for the view suggested here is not merely the problem of human immortality. Rather it is rooted in the larger question of the metaphysical status of the so-called "necessities"—propositions, properties, universals, and numbers. My concern is limited to properties, but one might be able to apply what I say here more generally.

The immortality of the human person in Christian thought is not the somewhat more full-blooded immortality found in the Greeks, or at least in Plato. Christian orthodoxy does not teach that the soul preexisted its beginning in the mother's womb.[1] Nor does Plato's soul depend on God. The immortality of Plato's soul seems to derive from the sort of being it is—a being like the forms. The soul is, so far forth in contemporary terms, a necessity. As a necessity, the soul is (minimally) simple, invisible, and eternal.[2] Plato's immortality is, apparently, everlasting and permanent and, as such, immortal in both temporal directions. There never was a time when the soul was not, just as there never was a time when the forms were not. Also, Plato makes a clear demarcation between the human body and the human soul, the former dissipating at death, the later continuing on in, presumably, the neighborhood of the forms. Christianity, arguably, makes no such demarcation. Although dualism has often been defended by theists, it is not at all clear that the human person can be so neatly divided up on scriptural grounds. It is, after all, as a resurrected human that Jesus returns to God. Christians hope for a bodily resurrection. Further, heaven is not the place where resurrected and redeemed humans dwell. Rather it is the new heaven and earth, arguably a physical place (metaphysically if not causally) related to the present one.

To draw out some thoughts about a metaphysical structure in which immutable immortality might be at home, my initial strategy is to reflect on Plato's argument for the natural immortality of the soul. Of course, Plato would not let me get away with the account of the soul found in the Christian view. His soul is immortal in both directions, the Christian soul is uni-directional in time. Also, as I've been using the notion of soul, I've remained neutral on what counts as essential to souls. It could include some sort of body, a view Plato would reject.

Plato's argument for the immortality of the soul can be understood as having three stages. The third rests directly on a contrast between the soul and the body and an attempt to align the former with the realm of the forms. I'll focus mainly on that aspect of his argument and only briefly

---

1. Some less orthodox groups teach this. I believe the Church of Jesus Christ of Latter Day Saints purports that human souls preexist life on earth. This is perhaps a little surprising given the Mormon emphasis on rejecting Greek thought about, say, the Trinity.

2. Exactly which features Plato thought the soul has is not actually as clear as I make it out. His is an argument from analogy or comparison. Which of the two worlds is the soul more like—the realm of the forms or the physical world? More like the former and so it is probably eternal. He explicitly discusses simplicity and seems to conclude that because the soul can't fall apart, rot, break apart, and so forth—because it has no parts—that it is like the forms and cannot (probably) be merely temporary. (In the *Republic*, Plato provides a tripartite view of the soul and thus seems to claim something contradictory to the idea in the *Phaedo* that the soul is simple, that is, without components or parts.)

Some Speculative Metaphysical Structure

touch on the other two stages. But I use it only as a springboard for the metaphysical framework I want to propose. I do not pretend to Platonic exegesis. The first stage of his argument derives from observing the widespread nature of alteration—just as cold comes from hot and hot from cold, sleeping from waking and waking from sleeping, so death comes from life and life from death. The second stage appeals to the apparent knowledge we have of things such as equality itself, knowledge that must have come, says Plato, from a previous life. Put these two stages together and we have life eternal in both temporal directions. A rejection of the first stage will only get us immortality prior to birth, something the Christian Scriptures do not support. Of course, the argument from alteration is rooted in reasoning from premises that are dubious at best. Not all change is cyclical. So these two stages of the argument strung together fail. At most they give us a soul existing prior to its birth in the body on earth. So no help for Christian theology there.

The third stage, sometimes called the affinity argument, argues from analogy between the two worlds of Plato—the world of the visible, changing appearances, and the world of the invisible, unchanging forms—by comparing the soul to each world. The soul (in Plato's clearly disembodiable sense, not the broader sense I want to use) being much more like the latter than the former provides for the probable conclusion that the soul is immortal like the forms. The forms are invisible, simple, unchanging, and eternal. Since he is arguing for the eternality of the soul, he can't appeal to eternity to show it immortal. So let's consider the others.

Is the soul invisible? Yes, or at least on dualist grounds. Is the soul unchanging? Well, maybe. That may depend on the other property I've listed, the soul's purported simplicity. The soul may be unchangeable because it is non-composite or simple. Simple things (like the forms) cannot fall apart, break apart, rot, or otherwise disintegrate. Thus, neither can the soul change if it too is non-composite or simple. But is it? Perhaps. I think we'd need to know a lot more about how Plato thought of simplicity than we do. But the real issue for present purposes is if we think of the soul as the essential aspect (or aspects) of the human person, and we don't exclude embodiedness as a concomitant essential property, then the soul would not be simple on those grounds alone. Bodies clearly aren't, perhaps even can't be, simple.

So I propose a slight shift in direction. Plato's forms, whatever else they might be in his thought, have come to be thought of as properties,

Appendix A

including essential properties. Properties, along with propositions, possible worlds, numbers, and so forth are now typically thought of by philosophers as abstract objects. Abstract objects are typically, though not always, thought to be non-temporal, non-spatial, and causally inert. So if the soul is like properties, then on contemporary grounds it would be non-temporal, non-spatial, and causally inert. But Plato's soul was anything but causally inert. It moved the body. This should not be a surprise, for in Plato's scheme the forms themselves were, in a significant way, the heart of the causal nexus that brings all concrete objects into existence.

Here we have a hint of how to bring Plato's insight about immortality into the Christian framework. Christians do not think, and have not since St. Augustine at least, that the forms float around mindlessly in "serene majesty" (in Alvin Plantinga's memorable phrase). The forms, whatever, else they are, are related to God in some special way. I'll say more about that below. Here I want only to note that if we are to suggest an argument for natural immortality that is Christian, it will need to be constructed against the backdrop of Christian theism. In that context, the soul is not like the forms, but like God. God is, arguably, not an abstract object, but rather the most concrete object of all. Yet God is a necessary being just as are numbers, propositions, and properties.

Plato, of course, did not think of the forms as causally inert. Nor, perhaps, should Christian philosophers. This is particularly true if we think of the forms as inseparable from God. But it is God, if anything, that is the causal source of all that is and we need to be clear that God is a concrete being capable of causal actions. But God is a special sort of concrete being, the being that is the ontological ground of all that is, including properties. But God also has properties. Now properties are typically thought of as abstract. What then is the relationship between God and abstracta?

The relationship between God, on the one hand, as a necessary but concrete being who is the fundamental source of all that is and, on the other hand, the other necessities—properties, propositions, numbers, etc.—is from a Christian point of view problematic.[3] God is supposed to be the one and only self-existent being. God's necessity is the fundamental feature of reality and from God's necessary being all other things come. But if abstract objects are, indeed, necessary, then we have to explain the relationship between God and abstract objects. I'm not going to take on the larger project

---

3. See Gould, ed. *Beyond the Control of God? Six Views on the Problem of God and Abstract Objects* for an extended discussion of various potions on God and abstract objects.

74

Some Speculative Metaphysical Structure

in detail. I will suggest, however, that abstracta may depend on God's being logically (not necessarily causally) and, as such, abstracta may exist only so far as God exists. Since there never was a time when God was not, so there never was a time when abstracta were not. On this account, it need not be the case that properties are themselves necessities. They could be simply strongly immutable entities (both enduring and immemorial), completely and utterly stable, but nevertheless contingent. They neither come into being nor cease to be; they are because logically they depend on God's being.

But I want to focus on a much smaller set of abstracta, viz. properties—Plato's forms. In particular, I want to think about those properties that can also be described as universals. Universals are properties typically thought of as multiply instantiable. We can minimally say of the relationship between God and universals that, like abstracta more generally, they may logically (but not necessarily causally) depend on God's being and hence there never was or will be a time when universals do not exist. I'll return to narrow that claim below.

Are souls like universals? Clearly not in all ways, for the soul is not multiply instantiable. Souls, in that regard, are not abstract objects, but more like God—concrete beings with properties. God has properties, some of which are multiply instantiable. God is not simply identical to divine properties. Further, souls are not like universals in being eternal in both directions as universals are typically thought to be (as abstracta).

How should the Christian philosopher think of universals? Perhaps by turning to what might seem an unlikely source of aid, the physicalist David Armstrong. Armstrong argues that universals are always instantiated. So there are no "free-floating" universals. Furthermore, for Armstrong, states of affairs are truth-makers for propositions. So, a's being F is the state of affairs in virtue of which "a is F" is true. Further, if "a is F" is true, a instantiates F-ness. Now Armstrong further claims that not every property reflects a universal; indeed, universals match up with the fundamental particles of science. Finally, he says that universals are instantiated somewhere, sometime. Since he is a physicalist, he will unpack "somewhere, sometime" strictly in physical terms. But in the middle of all this, he remains a realist about universals, a non-Platonic realist. Universals, however, are always and everywhere concretized and not, presumably, found floating around in mindless, majestic serenity.[4]

---

4. See Armstrong, *Nominalism & Realism*, vol. 1.

Appendix A

Now if we drop the Armstrongian commitment to physicalism, and his commitment to linking properties to fundamental particles, and allow for non-material objects to be concrete, we can allow for God to be a concrete object that instantiates various properties. So instead of saying that universals are instantiated somewhere, sometime, we might say more generally that they are instantiated by something, sometime.[5] If what it is to be a universal is for it to be multiply instantiable and, in fact, instantiated by something, sometime, then universals are always concretized. Here I must narrow my earlier suggestion that because God exists, universals exist. The most one could claim here, on the Armstrongian-inspired model, is that because God exists, the universals God instantiates exist. This parallels, in some ways, Armstrong's claim that there are some basic universals—universals attached to physically basic entities that are real—mass, for example. Insofar as Armstrong is a physicalist attempting to defend scientific realism, his basic ontological building blocks are states of affairs in which universals play a role. But universals would exist, on his view, only so long as there are physical things in virtue of which universals are concretized "somewhere, sometime." For the Christianized Armstrongian, universals would exist not fundamentally in the physical order but in God's being.

A final word about Armstrong. Armstrong's view of universals is, he claims, non-Platonic realism. Universals really exist. It's just that they are always concretized—instantiated somewhere, sometime. In certain ways, his view appears like Aristotle's, which seems to be that if there were, say, no things of which "being black" is predicated truly, there would be no universal property "being black." Universals would, so to speak, "come and go" as they are instantiated. On my modified Armstrong-inspired suggestions, God instantiates at least some properties, and if God's existence is necessary, then those properties—those universals—at least, do not "come and go." They would not exist at all if God didn't exist, but since God necessarily exists, so do those properties. That doesn't make them necessary, however. Some properties God has would be necessary while others might be strongly stable. God's sinlessness might fall into the latter category. God is strongly stably sinless because of other properties God has, say omniscience and omnipotence.[6]

---

5. There may be an issue here for those theists who consider God to be timeless. I don't believe God is timeless, but everlasting. Perhaps this description can be fixed up for the atemporalists among us.

6. See Morris for a discussion of this.

Some Speculative Metaphysical Structure

I mentioned above that the properties that God has may be basic, similar to the way in which Armstrong suggests that some properties of physical things are basic. Mass is a basic property in Armstrong's scheme. What might be basic in theism's scheme? Power, knowledge, wisdom, truth, love, and freedom, perhaps. When God creates the world with free agents capable of generating love, God acts in a way deeply consonant with the divine nature. Some properties that the created order instantiates are not instantiated by God in the divine self. They are created by God as the divinity works. Those properties may, in fact, be fundamentally stable, whether weakly or strongly. And here I'll go out on a speculative limb. Perhaps none of the properties the created order instantiates are necessities. Perhaps there are, indeed, no "free-standing" necessities at all. Perhaps, as I suggested above, only God instantiates basic universals and they are logically necessary only because God is a necessary being. All the properties instantiated by the created order are ultimately sustainingly contingent.

By that last term, I have in mind not merely that the created order need not have been, but that once it is created, God's presence, plans, and intentions cannot be logically separated from the created order. Hence, there are no essential properties, but rather there are various sorts of stable properties—enduring, immemorial, and immutable in Morris's sense. Although Morris does not deny the truth of necessary claims, he brings stable claims in alongside them to do various sorts of explanatory work. I want to push Morris's ideas further out. My fundamental reasons for this suggestion is that I think it comports well with the ultimate contingency of the world and it comports well with evolutionary theory, both for biology and physical cosmology. But I'll not attend to those reasons further here.

On this briefly described understanding, the forms are themselves permanent and stable because God is necessary or, less happily put, the forms are immortal because God is immortal. Free will, as instantiated by humans are like the properties God instantiates—immortal once instantiated, the difference being, of course, that human free will instantiations have a beginning whereas the universals associated with God do not.

My suggestion could even extend to numbers. It may be, then, as Morris suggests, that at least some features of numbers are stable properties, both strongly enduring and strongly immemorial. The number 3's being prime, for example. Why not count their very existence as such? The so-called "necessities" then are really contingent on God's being, but nevertheless, timelessly stable. Rather than being "necessities," they are "stabilities."

Appendix A

Properties, because they are "stabilities," are themselves stable and yet contingent on God's existence.

Given that sort of framework, if we limit our concern to properties that God instantiates and compare them to properties humans instantiate, we might find some feature that humans have that makes them "like the forms," as least insofar as they are both dependent on God for their being and, once having been made, they last forever. It's not hard to come up with properties—universals—shared by God and humans. Since God is all-knowing and instantiates that property, God automatically instantiates the property "being knowledgeable," a property humans have. Since God is all-powerful, God therefore instantiates "being powerful," as do humans. God, of course, has many of the properties God has of necessity in a way that humans do not. We are, ultimately, contingent, whereas God is not. On the model being suggested, however, the properties that might once have been considered essential to humans are merely rooted in God and the divine structure, with the result that the properties in virtue of which we are what we are are strongly stable and hence not intrinsic to us. This would be an even more radical version of the stable properties being extrinsic to us. Immortality would not depend on other essential properties such as free will, but all properties would be directly rooted in God's power and love.

Now nothing in my argument in the main text hangs on this further proposed ontology of properties. It might very well turn out that we do have a set of essential properties in virtue of which we are what we are. Nevertheless, it seems that immortality is not one of those essential properties. It finds its main support, if my argument is correct, in the essential property of free will and that, in turn, finds its support in God's nature and the divine plan for the universe. We are not immortal, hence, in the freestanding sense that Plato seems to have thought.

One of the reasons many people may reject Plato's affinity argument for immortality is that humans are concrete and we have come to think of the forms as abstract and therefore causally inert. On the model proposed here, forms—the universals—are always concretized. As such, they are not causally inert. This fits better with Christian theism overall, I believe, than with a full-court Platonism. God is a fundamental causal force in the universe and we humans mirror that activity. God's activity extends, then, to the universe through and through, including, ultimately, keeping humans from being merely mortal.

Some Speculative Metaphysical Structure

To get an argument for immutable immortality off the ground, one would have to show or make plausible, at least, that some enduring property or other is, once given a human, not capable of destruction. And this must be shown to be metaphysical fact, not merely the result of a moral obligation God has. As we've seen in chapter 5, free will may be a property that God cannot destroy without undermining God's own plan and nature, and it is a property, arguably, that is essential to human persons. Hence, human immortality flows from God's creative, causal role in the universe via an essential property humans have. Immortality is not essential to humans, but it is stable nonetheless.

Appendix B

Is Annihilation Worse Than Everlasting Torment?

Perhaps the most common argument against the traditional notion of the Christian hell is the disproportionality (or justice) argument. Since any punishment must be proportionate to the wrong-doing, and since human wrong-doing is finite in measure, then everlasting (that is, infinite), conscious torment (ECT) is out of proportion with the wrong-doing of sin. Therefore, hell understood as ECT is unjust. In contrast stands the status argument, which defends ECT. Because the status or nature of God is infinitely valuable (good, holy, and so forth), any wrong-doing against God deserves infinite (everlasting) punishment. Therefore, hell understood as ECT is just. A key difference between these arguments is the assumptions made about the effects of sin, which presumably flow from sin's nature, which in turn is linked to the measure of punishment deserved for that sin. The justice argument claims sin and/or its effects are finite, the status argument claims sin and/or its effects are infinite. Much turns, then, on what is meant by the terms *sin*, *finite*, and *infinite*. Does sin demand a finite or infinite punishment and what, exactly are finite and infinite punishments? A recent essay by James S. Spiegel compares two sorts of punishment for sin. My goal is to respond briefly to his claim that annihilation is worse punishment than ECT.

The disproportionality argument is used to suggest that God would be more just were recalcitrant sinners simply annihilated, perhaps after some time of conscious torment. Such a view is called annihilationism or conditionalism, where immortality is conditional on the appropriate response to

God. Spiegel attempts to turn the disproportionality argument on its head, arguing that annihilation is actually worse than ECT. Because annihilation is a worse punishment than ECT, he writes:

> Now the conditionalist can effectively meet the proportionality criterion by (a) accepting the notion that sinning against God warrants the most severe punishment possible and (b) proposing that annihilation is itself the greatest possible punishment. But this also means that if the conditionalist wants to continue to use the justice argument against traditionalism, she will need to alter it. For in granting the premise that sin deserves the greatest possible punishment, the conditionalist can no longer complain that ECT is disproportionate insofar as it is too severe. Rather, ... the situation reverses, as now the traditionalist doctrine must be construed as unjustly disproportionate to human sin because the punishment of ECT is not severe enough.[7]

The disproportionality argument fails to show that annihilationism is more just because less severe than ECT and hence more proportional to an individual's sin. Any disproportionality is due to ECT being too weak a punishment.

A general observation: The two arguments—the disproportionality and the status—use quite different measures. The disproportionality argument matches sin(s) to punishment(s) "one-to-one" in an almost arithmetical sense. Because the negative effects of sin seem finite (in number and quality), any damage done by sin—damage that needs to be "paid for" in punishment—is limited in scope. That limitation suggests that everlasting (infinite) punishment is too much. The status argument, in contrast, says that the damage done by sin is done to an infinitely valuable person—God—and hence is so bad that even a single offence against an infinite value deserves infinite punishment. Quantity doesn't seem to enter the picture at all. It's not obvious which view of the nature and effects of sin is the right view. One supposes that these conflicting intuitions on the nature of, and damage done by, sin are responsible for the different emphases in the arguments. If that is the case, then the arguments may be incommensurable, for they are comparing different notions of sin and its effects. While philosophers and theologians may eventually come to agreement on the nature and effects of sin, until they do, it seems that the conditionalist and the traditionalist may just have to agree to disagree.

---

7. Spiegel, "Annihilation," 246.

Appendix B

Nevertheless, Spiegel's argument is clever for it seems to give both parties in the debate what they have in view. On the one hand, if successful it gives the conditionalists what they want—annihilation understood as a punishment for sin, but one that does not make God a sadist. On the other hand, if successful, it gives the traditionalists what they want—justice in God's treatment of the recalcitrant unredeemed that is proportional to God's greatness.

We should note too that both arguments are defensive. The justice argument is defensive of a certain notion of God's justice, viz., God would never mete out more punishment than is actually deserved. The status argument is defensive of God's just nature in that the biblical descriptions of hell (and perhaps our Dante-inspired readings of the Christian Scripture) are shown to be quite just. So there is a common theme in both arguments: God's justice. It is this common belief—that God is just—that drives both arguments and that allows Spiegel's argument to include not a little touch of irony.

His argument allows the conditionalist to proclaim the annihilation of the recalcitrant unredeemed, but only on the condition that God appears even worse than on the traditionalist view, but proportionally just on the traditionalist's grounds of the infinite value of God. But the argument also allows the traditionalist to proclaim a level of punishment consistent with God's greatness, but only by upholding proportionality to God's nature and yet removing the punishment from the conscious realm in a permanent way. Part of the conditionalist's motivation is to make God seem less sadistic. Part of the traditionalist's motivation is to take the traditional account of hell—as rooted in the Bible's language—seriously and thus to make sure the punishment of a recalcitrant sinner is something of which she continues to be aware. Annihilation understood as an even worse punishment than ECT has the odd result of pleasing neither group.

It doesn't seem that the typical annihilationist will or should be happy to have won the day (or the eternity!) on Spiegelian grounds. Spiegel quotes John Wenham:

> Unending torment speaks to me of sadism, not justice. It is a doctrine which I do not know how to preach without negating the loveliness and glory of God. From the days of Tertullian it has frequently been the emphasis of fanatics. It is a doctrine which

makes the Inquisition look reasonable. It all seems a flight from reality and common sense.[8]

The typical conditionalist would follow Wenham in claiming that annihilationism is a more loving thing for God to do than punish the recalcitrant sinner forever consciously. To ratchet *up* the punishment from "mere" everlasting, but conscious, punishment to permanent cessation of consciousness altogether is not the goal of the annihilationist, presumably. They are interested in ratcheting *down* the punishment by looking for a kinder, gentler God, a God who is not committed to sadism. Still, the typical conditionalist doesn't want to lose God's justice in the discussion either.

For the traditionalist, however, the Spiegelian view of annihilation turns hell into something less than punishment—or less than biblical punishment—for punishment must be conscious. Presumably this idea is rooted in the traditional notion of hell as presented in some biblical texts. So this view also has the side-effect of requiring too much revisionist re-reading of the Christian Scripture, a complaint frequently brought against conditionalism in general. These problems—both for the traditionalist and the conditionalist—go away, however, if Spiegel's view is incorrect. I think, in fact, his suggestions are largely implausible.

Spiegel notes a framing observation about ECT. He writes:

> But supposing that the infinite goodness of God does require the greatest degree of punishment of sins, why assume that ECT is the option that properly satisfies this demand? Probably most make this assumption automatically because of the externality of the suffering of the damned implied in ECT. What could possible exceed infinitely long suffering? The first thing to note in response is that the temporal magnitude of ECT is never an actual infinite but only a potential infinite. . . . [W]hen speaking of ECT, one is always referring to something that is potentially infinite in the sense that it can continue forever—more moments may be added to the series indefinitely. But the series is never actually infinite.[9]

This is an important point for it is easy to speak fast and loose about infinite punishments that outstrip the finite nature and number of sins the recalcitrant unredeemed commit. So the disproportionality argument is not best understood as suggesting that the punishment of hell is infinite whereas

---

8 Wenham, "The Case for Conditional Immortality," 92, as quoted by Spiegel, "Annihilation," 242.

9. Spiegel, "Annihilation," 243.

Appendix B

the sin is finite. ECT may very well fit the wrong-doing in terms of both the punishment and crime being finite in number. There is no imbalance of an infinite number of punishing experiences balanced against a finite number of sins, since the infinite number of punishing experiences is never more than a potential infinite and so at any point in time remains finite.

However, even having recognized that hell involves only a potentially infinite series of events rather than an actual infinite one, a person might still press the disproportionality argument against ECT because the actual number of punishing experiences will at some point exceed the number of sins committed on earth. Yet that problem can be easily handled by a traditionalist. One continues to sin after death; one doesn't cease to be a sinner once in hell. If nothing else, one can imagine the recalcitrant unredeemed cursing God continually and hence the number of punishing experiences will never outrun the number of sins. But what these observations call attention to is a tendency to treat sin merely as a series of wrong actions. Yet sin has qualitative aspects as well as quantitative features. Sin is not merely actions, but a way of being. But then, goodness is not merely worthwhile actions, but a way of being. The distinction between actions and being suggests that punishment should be understood not merely as a series of negative experiences, but rather as an ontological loss of goodness. Perhaps, indeed, this sort of observation is behind some of Spiegel's argument. I believe, however, that these two ways of thinking of punishment are incommensurable.

Now to Spiegel's three reasons why annihilation is a more severe punishment than ECT. First, annihilation of the self is complete and final whereas ECT is neither complete nor final. Second, annihilation involves complete removal of goodness in a person whereas ECT does not. Third, annihilation eliminates an entire substance whereas ECT only eliminates certain qualities of the being and some vital relational facts and experiences. I'll take these in turn.

The first bit of evidence seems to rely on some slippery use of language. The term *final* is ambiguous between, on the one hand, "over" or "completed" and, on the other hand, "permanent." While Spiegel recognizes that God's judgment may be final (and hence ECT permanent), he suggests that it is ontologically and logically possible that the execution of the judgment is not. A cessation of suffering and even eternal redemption both remain open ontological and logical possibilities. But are they really possible, in either sense? I find the answer to turn on the ambiguity of the term *final*. Such ontological and logical possibilities would depend on God, once having judged a person, changing the divine mind. But surely God either won't or can't do that ontologically if the divine judgment is final in the permanent sense. And while there may be a possible world in which ECT ends, it wouldn't be the actual world. Otherwise God is a moral or epistemic failure in this world. Since God's being a moral or epistemic failure seems contrary to the divine nature, whence either the ontological or the logical possibility? The possibilities seem to appear only if Spiegel turns to use the other sense of "final"—the sense of "over" or "complete." By "over" or "complete" I mean something in the order of "having occurred in time." But a judgment having occurred in time does not entail that it was meant to be permanent. Perhaps God's judgment is more a temporary injunction than a final court decision. While I think the doors of hell may very well be locked from the inside so that some, perhaps even all, may leave by changing their minds, that only seems ontologically and logical possible if the divine judgment is not permanent, but rather simply "past but temporary." So it is not clear that when ECT and annihilation are compared that one is final and complete whereas the other is not. Perhaps both are final and complete; there is no returning from annihilation and there is no getting out of ECT.[10]

Spiegel's second reason claims that annihilation involves complete removal of goodness in a person in a way that ECT does not. Spiegel notes two ways in which we can understand this claim. Augustine suggested that a thing is good so far as it exists. On this view, goodness attends to any person who continues to exist, even those in hell. So annihilation is worse than ECT. Another way to understand the second reason is via the imago Dei. In hell, under the conditions of ECT, the recalcitrant unredeemed retain the divine image, for they remain essentially human. The loss of one's essence in annihilation, however, leads to the destruction of what is truly good in the human. I'll return to these momentarily, for I think the third reason Spiegel proffers is just another understanding of his second reason.

The third reason is that annihilation eliminates an entire being or substance whereas ECT only rids the person of certain qualities and some relational facts. What Spiegel has in mind in the former are positive or pleasant states of consciousness; in the latter he is thinking of fellowship with God and God's comforting presence. He writes that even the "complete and

---

10. If anything, annihilation might not be permanent, but only if one could maintain personal identity over a "gappy" existence. I'm skeptical of that possibility, however.

permanent loss of consciousness, while preserving the substance of a human being, would be more severe than ECT, since this would be to eliminate a fundamental goodness in the person and an essential aspect of her nature."[11] His point is that with ECT the punishment is essentially qualitative whereas with annihilation it is ontological. However, I'm hard pressed to see any significant difference between reason two and reason three. In losing the goodness of being or the image of God one is losing one's basic ontology. Thus it is with reason three. So it seems that Spiegel only proffers two reasons, not three, with the putative third reason being just another way of understanding the second reason. From here on, I'll refer only to his second reason, incorporating his third into the second.

It seems to me that, in some sense, Spiegel makes an important observation in his second reason. There is something of value—even great value—lost in annihilation that is not lost in ECT. But while there is a loss of value in the universe at the annihilation of an unredeemed person (whether we understand that value as existence, the imago Dei, or the entirety of being), it is a loss of value. A loss of value, however, need not, and perhaps cannot, be a punishment of the person in question. Spiegel recognizes this challenge when he notes that others have assumed that punishment must always be experienced.[12] He evidences the claim that experienced punishment is not the only sort of punishment by pointing to capital punishment. He writes:

> The analogy [between annihilation and capital punishment] is admittedly imperfect, but it is enough to show that the justice of a punishment is not entirely contingent upon one's conscious experience of it. It is enough that the person punished loses something valuable (which is the definitive factor on most retributive accounts of punishment). And whether one loses her earthly life or afterlife, these are the most extreme losses a human being can experience in either realm.[13]

I suggest that the analogy is not merely "imperfect." At best, if annihilation were a punishment, we are of two minds about it. At worst, the analogy doesn't work at all.

---

11. Spiegel, "Annihilationism," 244.
12. Here Spiegel refers to Saville, "Arguing with Annihilationism," and Bawulski, "Annihilationism, Traditionalism, and the Problem of Hell."
13. Spiegel, "Annihilationism," 245.

Let's take another analogy, one that also involves the cessation of life. Let's think of annihilation as parallel not to capital punishment but to euthanasia. In many euthanasia cases, especially those that occur at the conscious behest of the one dying, the cessation of one's earthly life is not taken to be an evil or a harm done, but rather the alleviation of evil or harm, sometimes even a positive good. It is certainly not punishment; and the attitude toward euthanasia cases is quite different than it is toward capital punishment. Now we can admit that in some general sense, death itself is a bad thing. The death of a person when all is well with that person is a bad thing—perhaps because it seems to us (barring a negative after-life) that one loses being, the imago Dei, or substance. But sometimes the cessation of the self is a welcomed event nonetheless. Given a choice between a life that is nasty, brutish, and long, and an early death, death is the "better" choice. But here we must be careful. While one might be able to compare apples to oranges, it is much more difficult to compare apples to space flight. So while one can recognize that death is bad taken strictly on its own grounds, sometimes it is a bad that has a good result. It is hard to see how to compare the loss of life or being with experienced, ongoing suffering, let alone everlasting suffering. They involve two quite different sorts of (dis-)value.

It is difficult to free ourselves of the language of experience. Note, for example, that Spiegel, at the very end of the most recent quotation, uses the term "experience" when he describes losing one's earthly being or postmortem loss of being. Likewise, Spiegel quotes James Cain approvingly when he explains suffering as the pains of loss and the pains of sense; the suffering of privation and a positive experiential kind of suffering.[14] However, "experience," "suffering," and "pain" are used in two fundamentally different ways in these quotations. One is clearly experiential and the other is ontological. The latter need not involve any conscious experience, pain, or suffering at all and the use of the "consciousness" terms is, arguably, metaphorical, rather than literal, in the ontological cases. This propensity to use the language of experience when we speak of values is difficult to shake and may influence the way we think of different sorts of value in the universe. Yet since at the loss of the self, there is no self to experience anything, the loss of the self in annihilation cannot be experienced (except the fear of loss, perhaps, in the time leading up to the annihilation). Nor can the loss of the

---

14. See Cain, "On the Problem of Hell," 356 as quoted in Spiegel, "Annihilationism," 245.

self in euthanasia be experienced and Spiegel admits the same for capital punishment. So while there is a loss, it is a loss to the universe or at least those remaining conscious aspects of it—God, other humans, and animals. But it is *not* a loss to the person who dies.

So while the loss of existence, the imago Dei, or substance is a loss, it is not a loss experientially *to the one who ceases to be*. It remains, however, a loss to the universe. God and the larger communion of the saints may be saddened by the loss, but the annihilated unredeemed cannot be. She has lost nothing because she no longer is a "she" at all; indeed, she is no longer anything at all. So it is with capital punishment. We may call it a punishment, but punishment, if it is to be a punishment of the individual human, seems to require that that *very same individual human* experiences it.

Two final points. First, it seems to me that Spiegel's entire discussion is misdirected. One cannot compare apples to oranges in any neutral way that suggests that one is better or worse than another. Similarly, one cannot compare the goodness of one's being to the experiences that may attend that being in any neutral way. If we take existence or being as a great-making property, the proper comparison is a being with existence and whatever other properties it may have and that same entity sans existence yet with those very same properties. To try to compare a life having both existence and ECT to a non-existent life is like comparing a bad film that has existence to a non-existent film. Which is better? I suspect we have no idea how to tell. We cannot compare, I suggest, the two spheres of existence/non-existence on the one hand and conscious eternal suffering on the other. But if we could compare a person who is suffering ECT and who happens to exist and that very same person suffering the very same ECT but who happens not to exist, I think we can safely say that it is worse to be the former than the latter. That, it seems, is the point of the mainstream conditionalist.

Second, let's return to the fact that annihilation is not taken by conditionalists—or need not be taken by them—as punishment at all. This should come as no surprise, for one central goal of many annihilationists is to preserve God's love, that is, to protect God's love from being downgraded by the apparent sadism that ECT suggests. Now of course, the conditionalist may want to protect God's justice too. But perhaps God's justice need not be protected. Indeed, perhaps annihilation simply is not an issue of justice at all. Since no human ever asked to be created in the first place, the recalcitrant unredeemed (by choice, action, or otherwise) may simply refuse the gift of existence, no matter how valuable it is. Given that, God need not punish unrepentant sinners. All God needs to do is to remove the gift. Or perhaps God need not do anything at all. Perhaps the gift, once cast aside, simply rots away. In either case, the matter isn't one of justice, but rather one of metaphysical causation.

In summary, I don't find Spiegel's evidence to be strong enough. Further, it seems that annihilation cannot be compared to ECT at all. ECT is supposed to be a form of justice whereas annihilation is simply a natural result of refusing a gift, albeit a gift from God.

Appendix C

Soul Euthanasia and the Emptying of Hell

Hell being permanently filled is the main tradition in Christianity. As an alternative to everlasting, conscious punishment, some theologians and philosophers are drawn to the view that the recalcitrant unredeemed human soul simply ceases to be at some point, whether through God's choice or through the wasting away of the individual person.[1] Such a view is often called "annihilationism" and it is grounded in conditional immortality. I've argued against this view on philosophical grounds in the main part of this book. Another minority view exists, however, which does not allow soul cessation. That view is post-death universalism. I'll explore this through comparing various sorts of soul euthanasia. Fortunately for someone who argues against annihilationism as I've done and who finds eternal conscious punishment unconscionable, at least two versions of soul euthanasia set the stage for the recalcitrant unredeemed to return to God. Although hell cannot be emptied by soul euthanasia, it can be emptied by a post-hell universalism.

I prefer the terms *soul cessation* and the narrower term *soul euthanasia* to *annihilationism*. Soul cessation includes soul euthanasia, but also includes other sorts of end-game accounts for the soul. Furthermore, and as is consistent with my use through the book, I take the term *soul* to represent whatever the essence of a human person is so that the end of the soul is the end of the specific, particular, human person. Section I lays out various end-game accounts of the human person in this life. Section II explores various models of soul euthanasia. Given the evidence of the book for the

---

1. So C. S. Lewis et al.

claim that soul cessation is not possible, it seems that hell cannot be emptied via soul euthanasia. However, I argue that the recalcitrant unredeemed, in attempting to escape hell through their own soul cessation, come to realize their own dependence on God and turn, in a first step, at any rate, toward redemption. Section III concludes with some final reflections on suicide.

I

We can think of soul cessation as parallel to the cessation of life on earth. Earthly death comes in at least these ways: death by natural cause, death by accidental cause, death by murder, death by suicide, and death by euthanasia. There are many subtleties attaching to these various sorts of deaths. In some sense, all deaths are from natural causes for our bodies simply don't last forever. In every case, something interferes with those aspects of our bodily functions required to sustain life leading to life's end. A murder with a gun interferes with our body's normal function as clearly as does cancer. By "natural cause," however, I'll mean roughly what is meant in obituaries, viz., that no foul play, intentional killing, or accidental killing was involved in the cessation of life. When someone dies of natural causes, no human brings it about knowingly or directly. The person simply dies because that is what happens in nature.

Death by accidental cause, such as falling tree limbs, car accidents, and so forth, are picked out as distinct from natural causes because had the accident not occurred or had the person been at a different location at the time, etc., she would not have died. That is, she would not have died at that time had she not been involved in the accident. If one counts falling tree limbs as natural events, then in some sense, as noted earlier, such deaths are also from natural causes. The point I'm making is simply that something occurs to the person due to "external" events, events not directly tied to the natural or normal flow of events within the body. This point remains somewhat unclear, however, for sometimes a person dies of natural causes because he is infected from "outside" by a virus, let's say. We don't typically refer to those deaths as "accidental." Instead, we think of them as natural. Deciding what is natural and what is accidental may be a little dicey. Nevertheless, for the purposes here, the basic distinction is intuitively clear and while we might fuss about the details of certain cases, nothing of importance hangs on deciding those cases.

Appendix C

Death by murder, suicide, and euthanasia fall outside both the "natural" and the "accidental" descriptors. The reason is clear, for each of these sorts of deaths require some sort of intentional action either by oneself or another human person. They are in that sense neither natural nor accidental. The one exception is perhaps a sort of euthanasia in which the person is dying (of natural or accidental causes) and the person simply decides not to do anything to prevent the natural course of death. Here we need the further commonly made distinction between passive and active euthanasia. Although still not entirely clear, the distinction is roughly this: Active euthanasia is the intentional, "positive" act of bringing about a person's death when that person will die soon naturally otherwise (but perhaps in great pain). Passive euthanasia, in contrast, can be described as the refusal to act in a manner that would otherwise sustain a life that will end soon due to natural (or accidental) causes. Passive euthanasia is distinguished from natural death simply because there are things one could do to extend the dying person's life that one chooses not to do. That makes the death at least slightly more intentional than a merely natural death (when nothing else could be done). Thus what distinguishes natural (and accidental) from other deaths is the involvement of some human choice.

In addition to the passive/active distinction, it is common to distinguish between self- and other-inflicted euthanasia, as well as self-determined and proxy-determined. There are eight sorts of cases:

1. Self-determined, self-inflicted passive;
2. self-determined, self-inflicted active;
3. self-determined, other-inflicted passive;
4. self-determined, other-inflicted active;
5. proxy-determined, self-inflicted passive;
6. proxy-determined, self-inflicted active;
7. proxy-determined, other-inflicted, passive;
8. proxy-determined, other-inflicted, active.

To begin with the easiest case, 1 is perhaps paradigmatic of euthanasia. It is typically thought to be within one's rights under end-of-life conditions to be able to refuse aid with the continuance of one's life. To be made comfortable, yes. But the refusal of something that will continue one's life in the face of inevitable death seems to most people something a person is within her rights in choosing. 2 is more complicated, but a good many people think 2 is a morally viable option as well. Indeed, sometimes the active approach to one's own death is preferable in terms of lessening suffering than a passive approach. So let's grant, for the sake of the present argument, that 1 and 2 are morally acceptable.[2]

Turning now to 7 and 8, the door opens to potential abuse. That is, in 7 and 8 not only is the decision not made by the suffering person, but it is enacted by the proxy. The way to avoid potential abuse lies along the path of having clear criteria for proxy decisions to be enacted. What counts as a true proxy may involve some controversy, but it seems to include at least the following. The person represented by the proxy must give prior "sound body and mind" permission and, in the case of a decision about death, the represented person must be incapable of deciding at the point of the decision about death for her- or himself. Typically, this is because the represented person has ceased to function at a neurological/mental level so as to be capable of making a well-informed choice. In effect, she made the choice earlier and directed the proxy to carry it out. Should these conditions not be met, we call 7 and 8 cases of murder. But given that 7 and 8 are

---

2. Although many of us want to treat 1 and 2 as euthanasia cases, and to thus distinguish them from suicide, nevertheless 1 and 2 may be, strictly speaking, cases of suicide. They are, in short, the bringing to an end *one's own* life. Now one might suggest that 1 and 2 are distinguishable from suicide because in 1 and 2 the person is facing more or less immediate cessation of life anyway and one is simply quickening the inevitable for a good reason. However, this only seems to provide a different reason for suiciding, rather than making these sorts of euthanasia actually distinguishable from other cases of suicide. We might thus say that suicide overlaps with euthanasia insofar as the person suiciding takes her or his action to be a means of bringing about a quicker end than would normally occur. When these deaths occur because of deep pain or suffering, it can be hard to tell them from cases of active (or even passive) self-determined euthanasia. Even the slow death from alcoholism or drug-abuse might be viewed as self-medication eventually leading to one's death. Nothing in what I've said here, however, tells us when a suicide is legitimate morally or when it is not. This last comment itself is meant to leave open the issue of whether suicide is morally evaluable. Negative moral judgments that censure suicide are generally unpopular these days. I do not wish to wade into that difficult territory. Most of us think the suicides of those not about to die anyway to be unhappy, sad events. Whether we want to add moral censure to the act of suicide is something beyond such judgments. Typically we don't want to add to the deceased person's family and friends' grief at the loss of life any additional judgments. Nor do we want to add to the psychological burden of someone who has attempted but failed to suicide. Love, perhaps, dictates this more generous spirit. My main point here is not to enter the fray, but rather to note simply that some suicides seem clearly morally acceptable, while there is a question about the remaining ones. I intend only to work with those that seem fairly clearly morally acceptable, viz., those we refer to as euthanasia.

Appendix C

not against the will of the one dying—that is, in cases of true proxies—they should be treated morally just like 1 and 2. In true proxy cases, the proxy functions are the moral equivalent (so far as the choice is concerned) of the person the proxy represents. So long as true proxies are possible, we can treat 7 and 8 as rising and falling with 1 and 2.

3 and 4 are often referred to as "assisted suicide." They are suicide because the choice is made by the one who dies, but assisted because the other person brings about the events, or at least the salient physical ones, leading to the death. They are not murder, even though an agent other than the dying person is involved. In effect, the other person acts as a (partial) proxy, not in making the decision, but in bringing the decision to fruition. Again, if the partial proxy is a true one, and no malintent or conflict of interest is involved, such cases are treated more or less as the others thus far discussed. In terms of complexity, we might say there is a range from 1 and 2 through 3 and 4 to 7 and 8. Nevertheless, morally, the basic idea is that the person who is dying makes the choice in principle.

We can turn now to consider 5 and 6. So long as we limit the cases to true proxy cases—where another person has the clear and final right to choose about another's end of life, including the explicit permission of the person the proxy represents—5 and 6 seem incoherent. If a person were capable of acting (whether passively or actively) to bring about the end of her life, no proxy could legitimately be said to have a right to make the decision. No one could sign over the right to make the choice to end life to a proxy so long as the person being represented was able to make the decision to end herself.

Nevertheless, one can imagine someone deciding that she didn't want to ever make an end-of-life decision and setting up a proxy to make the decision for her, all the while intending to bring about the death-deed by herself once another person made the choice. While this seems possible, it has low probability. But there is a deeper issue here. There is an argument against even the possibility of letting another choose what to do about one's end of life so long one is conscious and able to decide for oneself. It is parallel to the argument that one cannot freely give oneself into total slavery to another. The reason one can't sign oneself into total slavery is that it is an ontological impossibility. The intuition here seems to be that because one is by nature free, one cannot by one's own choice, cease being free. One cannot become an automaton under the total control of another and still remain human; one's humanity ceased to be upon being made an automaton. Signing oneself into slavery is a way of signing oneself into an ontological change one isn't capable of accomplishing while remaining free. There are no willing slaves, in short. Insofar then as signing over one's right to make choices about the end of one's own life parallel that of making oneself a slave, no one could actually do so. One can only give permission for someone else to make the choice about one's own end of life when it is done before one becomes incapable of making the decision for oneself and the proxy is granted only on the contingency that one changes from a deliberative state to one where one cannot and will not be able to make one's own choice (permanent coma or other similar circumstances). On those grounds, 5 and 6 seem impossible.

II

Let's turn now to cases of soul euthanasia. For convenience, let's call soul euthanasia cases "euthanasia*" and number them parallel to the eight euthanasia cases discussed above also with a "*". Let's compare. Beginning with 1 and 2, a person chooses one's own end and thus in 1* and 2* one would choose one's own soulish end. Furthermore, one brings about one's own end in both cases. Finally, just as in 1 and 2 where the end is brought about by different means in the two cases, so in 1* and 2*, the end is brought about by different means. In the case of 1*, soul cessation would be a "wasting away" of one's soul that occurs "naturally" or "on its own" because one no longer "feeds" the soul. This is similar to C. S. Lewis' suggestion that someone may cease being a grumbler and become a mere grumble.[3] In 2*, one actively "kills" one's soul by one's "own hand."

There are two important differences between euthanasia and euthanasia* cases. The first is a general one in that when the latter cases require a proxy, that proxy is always God. The second difference between euthanasia and euthanasia* is that in the former there is generally nothing (typically) to stop one from both deciding to end one's life and inflicting the means of doing so. Where the dying person is both the decision maker and the inflicter, all things being equal, one can bring about one's earthly demise. As I suggested in the argument in section I, however, in euthanasia* cases it's not clear that the cessation of being is in fact metaphysically possible at one's own hand. While one can cause one's body to cease operating, it's

---

3. Lewis, *The Great Divorce*, 74–75.

less clear how one might cause one's soul to cease being, whether actively or passively.

How might one defend the idea that no human can metaphysically cause her own cessation? An argument to that end was presented in chapter 4, proceeding in general like this: Just as humans have no say over their creation, so they have no say over their permanent cessation. The creation and substance of a human person is due entirely to God. A human qua human can no more be the cause of its own end then it can be the cause of its own beginning. It seems entirely in the hands of God. Unlike with the cessation of an earthly human existence, the cessation of a human soul is permanent. The former is not really cessation, but only a change in venue. Perhaps one goes from this earthly mode of being to a more "stripped down" essential version of one's self. Or perhaps one ultimately is resurrected. But in either case, one does not truly cease to be at bodily death. In the case of the permanent cessation of the human soul, however, there is no resurrection or continuation in another form. One's essence is permanently gone. We humans exist entirely within the causal, sustaining web of God's love and power. Hence, while one might wish to cease to be, it's not more than a wish over something that is not in one's control. So it's not at all up to us to bring about our own, permanent cessation. Just as we have no power or influence over whether we are created in the first place, so it seems that we don't have the power or influence to cause our own (or anyone else's) permanent cessation. That's not the sort of being we are. We are contingent, but cannot cease to be under our own power.

Now if we cannot cause, metaphysically, our own cessation, then 3* and 4* may be the next best alternative. Perhaps only God can (metaphysically) cause the soul to cease to exist even if the decision is left to us. In 3* and 4* an individual makes the choice, but needs another party—God—to bring about the demise. Now if there are reasons why God cannot bring about the cessation, then 3* and 4* won't allow for soul cessation either. But God cannot morally bring about the demise of a soul even if God could bring it about metaphysically—so goes the argument in section I. It appears, then, that 1* through 4* are not possible routes to soul cessation. Soul cessation is not viable in any of those cases.

It should be observed, however, that as the recalcitrant unredeemed soul moves through options 1* and 2* the soul will surely observe that even though her free will is vast, it is not able to do any and everything it would like. Eventually the hellish person will realize that in cases 1* and 2* the soul cannot bring about its own end. She'll turn to 3* and 4* then, only to discover that that way out of hell won't work either. God is metaphysically obliged to keep such a valuable thing as free will in existence. Free will as capacity is so valuable that God keeps all created humans in permanent existence, no matter how bad that existence may be otherwise. So God simply isn't going to act on the human soul's request. It's making a bad choice of such magnitude that although God generally lets human free will take its course, the divine love won't let it deprive itself of its own being. At this point, the soul will recognize that God's will cannot be bent to the soul's. That brings the soul in hell finally to the realization that one depends on God.

Scripture repeatedly tells us to align our will with God's will. Or even more poignantly in this case, to trust God to do the best for us. In a sense, something similar happens in earthly proxy cases. While of course an earthly person turning over her decision to a proxy will ask the proxy to do what it is the person represented wills, one must have a great deal of trust (and it's usually all written down in legally binding agreements). In giving one's will over to God's will, one's trust is much greater than anything found among earthly inhabitants and their proxies. Indeed, given God's commitment to the value of instantiated human free will, God will not ever go along with the human's request for soul cessation. Hence begins the soul's journey back toward an appropriate relationship with God.

We can turn to other cases now. In 7* and 8*, God acts as a proxy and chooses to end the soul of the recalcitrant unredeemed. But free will is, as noted, incredibly valuable. As noted in the main text, this is indicated by the way we treat free will in discussions of the problem of evil. It is so valuable that it is the key to overcoming the challenge of evil being laid at God's feet. If human free will was valuable enough to allow for God to make humans in the first place, with all the risk of the great evils that we've generated, then it seems God's risk-taking in creating free humans makes us incredibly valuable. Because of these reasons, it's not at all clear that God can metaphysically destroy something of such great value, even at a human free-will request. Better for God not to have created at all, one might suppose, than to destroy what is created at great expense both to humans and to the divine being itself (in the work of Jesus). But God did create and instantiate free will in humans.

All this points up another significant difference between euthanasia and euthanasia*. In euthanasia cases, the decision to have a proxy in place is made "ahead of time," while one is fully conscious and able to make the decision and the results of that decision await circumstances in which one can no longer actually make a decision for oneself. There seems to be no hellish parallel, for presumably there is no time at which the soul is without consciousness and free will so as to be unable to make the decision. Presumably in the afterlife, a soul is always free and capable of making such decisions. Even if we live in a resurrected state in the afterlife, presumably no damage can be done to the body so as to make it impossible for one to make a free and conscious decision. So it is difficult to imagine what would have to be the case for God to have the "right" to make the decision for us. So 7* and 8* seem impossible for the requirements, for a true proxy can't be met.

Finally, 5* and 6* seem to face the same sort of difficulty in the afterlife as their parallels on earth do, viz., it's not clear that humans qua humans can in principle consciously sign away their free will and still be free. In this case, however, that seems to be exactly what is needed. Since the goal is to bring about the cessation of one's soul, that is, the cessation of one's very being as a human, then a soul's giving up one's self-determination to another is precisely what it would take to cause one's own end. Yet there is something peculiar about 5* and 6*, and the logic of the earthly and afterlife versions of 5 and 6 are not analogous. The reason the earthly version doesn't work is because one cannot both be responsible for the choice to end one life and not be responsible at the same time. One cannot cease being free to make the choice to end one's life and yet still be free. In 5* and 6*, however, one gives the decision over to God to whom one owes one's existence in the first place. But even granting that, if the anti-soul-cessation argument is right then God is metaphysically obliged to keep the person in existence because of her inherent value. Not even God would be able to let a human bring about his soul cessation. Somewhat surprisingly, however, that isn't what would result from a human person asking God to allow one's soul cessation in 5* and 6*.

One is in hell, presumably, for not being willing to recognize the role God has in one's very existence—one's dependence on God. But if one reaches the point where one would be willing to ask God to bring about one's cessation—perhaps even begging God for that end to come about—then one is beginning to recognize the relationship between oneself and the divine. That, in turn, is the first step toward a proper relationship with God. Here I think it is not a stretch to suppose that the people in hell are much more fully aware of their dependence on God than perhaps anyone on earth is. Perhaps this awareness is fundamental to hell because one's sense of being is stripped down to the essentials. Hence, while the awareness is perhaps brought about by negative circumstance alone, it may very well be a richer, more powerfully motivating awareness than a given individual experiences while alive on earth. So it is not unreasonable to think that one's willingness to ask God to be one's proxy in bringing about one's end while one is conscious, alive, and free in hell turns out to be the first step out of hell. It is the first step toward fully recognizing one's entire dependence on God.

At this point, one might suggest that the people in hell might never reach the place where they would be willing to ask God to be their proxy in this (or any other) way and so hell remains forever inhabited. In response, all the other paths out of the suffering of hell (whatever it may be) are blocked. One cannot both choose to cease to be and bring it about. Neither can anyone be one's proxy in choosing to cease to be and cause one's cessation. Here an appeal to Bernard Williams's and other similar arguments against the unpleasantness of immortality come into play.[4] Immorality without God is banal, boring, and without purpose, except perhaps to keep making free choices. Having reached this realization, the recalcitrant unredeemed will freely choose the path out via euthanasia*. Once realizing that the paths are all blocked it seems everyone will choose to recognize God as the source of their being and substance and hence begin the long journey out of hell. While one can imagine some being so recalcitrant as to reject even this sort of reliance on God, it seems to me quite unlikely that any human will be so recalcitrant.

III

I close with a brief reflection on suicide by Emily Esfahani Smith, who in turn quotes G. K. Chesterton. The quotation is about earthly suicide, but the comments seem to lend themselves even more strongly to soul suicide.

> The rise in suicide has been accompanied by a loss of the moral questions that once surrounded it. G. K. Chesterton was one of our last full-throated critics of suicide. His insistence that suicide is immoral sounds strange to our individualistic ears: "Not only is suicide a sin, it is the sin," Chesterton wrote: "It is the ultimate

---

4. See Williams, "The Makropulos Case."

Appendix C

and absolute evil, the refusal to take an interest in existence; the refusal to take the oath of loyalty to life. The man who kills a man, kills a man. The man who kills himself, kills all men; as far as he is concerned he wipes out the world." Chesterton goes on to say that the act of suicide is selfish: "A suicide is a man who cares so little for anything outside him, that he wants to see the last of everything." It would be difficult to imagine anyone writing such a polemic today. We do not consider suicide the moral catastrophe that people like Chesterton once thought it was.[5]

Chesterton obviously took suicide to be not merely morally serious but morally wrong—a great evil, even. Let's apply Chesterton's reasoning to soul suicide, of which all the cases of euthanasia* discussed above are arguably a species, even the assisted ones.

Chesterton says suicide is evil—indeed the sin of all sins—for what appear to be two basic reasons. First, one who suicides refuses to take an interest in anything but himself—existence, life, what is outside himself. Second, in killing himself he kills all people, something worse than "merely" killing another person. Perhaps, in the end, these reasons can't be separated. In suiciding, because one cares so little for anything outside oneself—existence, life, other people, the world—one wants to bring it all to an end. If we apply this not merely to earthly existence but existence in toto, then the situation is painted on a larger canvas. Soul suicide is the end of all, even God. Or so the soul suicide believes. But in trying to obtain the goal of soul euthanasia one will come to recognize the reality of not only other people and the value of God's created order but also the absolute centrality of God's sustaining love for us all, even those of us who have a long tour of duty in hell.[6]

---

5. Smith, "The Catastrophe of Suicide."

6. I want to thank Phil Smith for comments and discussions about this appendix. But I also want make a pastoral comment about suicide, earthly or otherwise. I don't believe Chesterton gets the whole picture right and the reason why negative moral judgments have fallen on hard times may have good reason behind them. That every person who suicides cares for nothing but himself is probably not true. Psychologically many people who suicide intend to help others—they don't want to be a burden any longer. At least, that is part of what is going on. So the reasons for suicide are complex and not so easily summarized in a couple of sentences. On the other hand, much of what Chesterton says does seem to apply to afterlife cases of soul cessation. One of the things missing in the understanding of free will as it is tied to self-interest is that on the Christian scheme of things we are not, in the end, entirely self-interested. Here I refer the reader to my unpublished "Agape, Altruism, and the Communion of the Saints." One might also consider the wisdom of Father Zosima in Dostoesky's *The Brothers Karamazov*. Zosima says that

Soul Euthanasia and the Emptying of Hell

In his fascinating reflections on ultimate questions, Bryan Magee writes:

> Schrodinger wrote that consciousness is a singular of which the plural is unknown, but I find myself reflecting that he should have added "and unknowable, though we know it to exist. Knowing it is a form of consciousness attributed to God." When I die this unique empirical world of my knowledge and experience (and memories) will come to an end. What happens then will depend on the relationship, if there is one, between, on the one hand, me and my empirical world taken together, reciprocal as they are, and on the other hand whatever exists independently of them. It could be that I and my empirical world relapse into nothingness. But this is not certain. What presents itself to me now as nothingness might be as deceptive in this as was the empty air around me before I switch on my pocket radio, or the visual world to a congenitally blind man about to get his sight. I am not confident about this—in fact, I am exceedingly doubtful—but the possibility exists.[7]

Magee's reflections, as skeptical as they are of religious belief, point toward something parallel with Chesterton's comments about suicide. When I die, says Magee, the empirical world that is unique to me will cease to be. The earthly suicide takes it that in his ending his life, he ends everything—the whole empirical world goes with him. For the soul suicide, something similar must be the thought. But it is precisely here that the recalcitrant unredeemed comes face to face with the "second hand" of Magee's description: whatever it is that exists independently of my consciousness and its empirical world. But as Magee notes, knowing the consciousness of others is, in fact, the province of God. When the recalcitrant unredeemed finally turns to God to ask God to "end it all" for the finite conscious suffering in hell, it seems that she or he is taking the first step to realizing that soul suicide is not the answer. God is. Thus, the possibility is open for hell to be emptied, not by soul cessation, but by the ever-present social relationship between God and the free human soul. When the recalcitrant unredeemed turn to ask for God's help in ending it all, they cannot help but take the first

---

hell is the inability to love. On that score, those in hell are without community and the turn toward God that I've suggested may be simply the recognition that one wants to love but that love can't occur without God. In short, I do not know that I agree entirely with Chesterton on suicide. His argument has not sat comfortably with me in the years that have passed since my late wife's suicide. She, I believe, was longing not for the end of all, but to see the face of God.

7. Magee, *Ultimate Questions*, 68.

step toward recognizing their dependence on God. God's love, far from serving up the requested end of the soul, sustains the soul long enough so that he may turn, finally, from seeing himself as the center of the "empirical world"—indeed, the center of all—toward the God who reveals true love to the lonely recalcitrant. So hell cannot be emptied by soul euthanasia, but it can be emptied by those who want to empty it. The grace of a loving God wins.

Works Cited

Armstrong, David. 1978. *Nominalism & Realism—Universals & Scientific Realism, Vol. 1.* Cambridge: Cambridge University Press, 1978.

———.*Universals.* Boulder, CO: Westview, 1989.

Bawulski, S. 2010. "Annihilationism, Traditionalism, and the Problem of Hell." *Philosophia Christi* 12 (2010) 61–79.

Brandyberry, James Kenneth. "Important Forgotten History: The Roots of Opposition to Conditionalism." In *A Consuming Passion: Essays on Hell and Immortality in Honor of Edward Fudge*, edited by Christopher M. Date and Ron Highfield, 245–56. Eugene, OR: Pickwick, 2015.

Cain, James. "On the Problem of Hell." *Religious Studies* 38 (2002.) 355–62.

Date, Christopher M., and Ron Highfield, eds. *A Consuming Passion: Essays on Hell and Immortality in Honor of Edward Fudge.* Eugene: Pickwick, 2015.

Date, Christopher M., Gregory S. Stump, and Joshua W. Anderson, eds. *Rethinking Hell: Readings in Evangelical Conditionalism.* Eugene, OR: Cascade, 2014.

Despain, David. "How to Achieve 'Biological Immortality' Naturally." *Kurzweil Accelerating Intelligence.* December 6, 2010. http://www.kurzweilai.net/how-to-achieve-biological-immortality-naturally.

Edwards, Paul, ed. 1997. *Introduction to Immortality.* Amherst, NY: Prometheus, 1997.

Fudge, Edward. *The Fire That Consumes: A Biblical and Historical Study of the Doctrine of Final Punishment.* Eugene: Cascade Books, 2011.

Gould, Paul, ed. *Beyond the Control of God? Six Views on the Problem of God and Abstract Objects.* New York: Bloomsbury, 2014.

Guadin, Sharon. "Nanotech Could Make Humans Immortal by 2040, Futurist Says." *Computer World from IDC.* October 1, 2009. http://www.computerworld.com/article/2528330/app-development/nanotech-could-make-humans-immortal-by-2040--futurist-says.html.

Hughes, Philip E. "Is the Soul Immortal?" In *Rethinking Hell: Readings in Evangelical Conditionalism*, edited by Christopher M. Date, Gregory S. Stump and Joshua W. Anderson, 185–97. Eugene, OR: Cascade, 2014.

Kane, Robert. *A Contemporary Introduction to Freewill.* Oxford: Oxford University Press, 2005.

Lewis, C. S. *The Great Divorce.* New York: Macmillan, 1946.

———. *The Weight of Glory: And Other Addresses.* Grand Rapids: Zondervan, 2001.

Works Cited

Magee, Bryan. *Ultimate Questions*. Princeton: Princeton University Press, 2016.

Marshall, Christopher D. "Divine and Human Punishment in the New Testament." In *Rethinking Hell: Readings in Evangelical Conditionalism*, edited by Christopher M. Date, Gregory S. Stump and Joshua W. Anderson, 207–27. Eugene, OR: Cascade, 2014.

Mavrodes, George. "Religion and the Queerness of Morality." In *Rationality, Religious Belief, and Moral Commitment: New Essays in the Philosophy of Religion*, edited by Robert Audi and William J. Wainwright, 213–26. Ithaca, NY: Cornell University Press, 1986.

Morris, Thomas V. "Properties, Modalities, and God." *The Philosophical Review* XCIII.1 (1984) 35–55.

Pinnock, Clark H. "The Destruction of the Finally Impenitent." In *Rethinking Hell: Readings in Evangelical Conditionalism*, edited by Christopher M. Date, Gregory S. Stump, and Joshua W. Anderson, 56–73. Eugene, OR: Cascade, 2014.

Rosenbaum, Stephen. "How to be Dead and Not Care." In *The Metaphysics of Death*, edited by John Martin Fischer, 119–34. Palo Alto, CA: Stanford University Press, 1993.

Saville, A. "Arguing with Annihilationism: An Assessment of the Doctrinal Arguments for Annihilationism." *Scottish Bulletin of Evangelical Theology* 24 (2006) 65–90.

Smith, Emily Esfahani. "The Catastrophe of Suicide." *New Criterion*. n.d. www.newcriterion.com.

Spiegel, James S. "Annihilation, Everlasting Torment, and Divine Justice." *International Journal of Philosophy and Theology* 76 (2015) 242–46.

Swinburne, Richard G. "The Future of the Totally Corrupt." In *Rethinking Hell: Readings in Evangelical Conditionalism*, edited by Christopher M. Date, Gregory S. Stump, and Joshua W. Anderson, 234–44. Eugene, OR: Cascade, 2014.

Talbott, Thomas B. *The Inescapable Love of God*. 2nd ed. Eugene, OR: Cascade, 2014.

Travis, Stephen H. "The Nature of Final Destiny." In *Rethinking Hell: Readings in Evangelical Conditionalism*, edited by Christopher M. Date, Gregory S. Stump, and Joshua W. Anderson, 44–47. Eugene, OR: Cascade, 2014.

Vlastos, Gregory. "Plato on Knowledge and Reality." In *Platonic Studies*, 374–81. 2nd ed. Princeton: Princeton University Press, 1973.

Wenham, John. "The Case for Conditional Immortality." In *Rethinking Hell: Readings in Evangelical Conditionalism*, edited by Christopher M. Date, Gregory S. Stump and Joshua W. Anderson, 74–97. Eugene, OR: Cascade, 2014.

Williams, Bernard. "The Makropulos Case: Reflections on the Tedium of Immortality." In *Problems of the Self*, 82–100. Cambridge: Cambridge University Press, 1973.

Williams, Margery. *The Velveteen Rabbit*. New York: Doran, 1922.

Wright, Nigel G. "A Kinder, Gentler Damnation?" In *Rethinking Hell: Readings in Evangelical Conditionalism*, edited by Christopher M. Date, Gregory S. Stump and Joshua W. Anderson, 228–33. Eugene, OR: Cascade, 2014.

Yourgrau, Palle. "The Dead." In *The Metaphysics of Death*, edited by John Martin Fischer, 137–58. Palo Alto, CA: Stanford University Press, 1993.

Index

annihilationism, x, 19, 26, 28, 53, 55
arminian, 32
Armstrong, David, 75, 76
calvinist, 32

Chesterton, G., K., 99, 100
consciousness, 18

death, 3, 5, 8, 9, 10, 15, 20, 90
disproportionality argument, 80

eschatology, x
eternal conscious punishment, 66, 80ff
euthanasia, types of, 92
existence, 4, 6, 7

freedom-as-capacity, 40, 41, 42, 49, 55, 68, 69
freedom-as-choice, 40, 41, 42, 49, 56
freewill, 16, 17, 37, 38, 60, 66

God, x, 10, 30, 31, 32, 38, 39, 40, 41, 43, 45, 57, 60, 67, 102

heaven, ix, x
hell, ix, x, 49, 51

immortality, ix, x, 1, 2, 26–27
    conditional, x, 23–25, 26, 28, 52
    functional, 21
    immutable, 51–76

natural, 25, 51
personal, 2, 3

Lewis, C.S., xiii, 45, 47
love, 63, 64

MacTaggart, ix memory, self-identifying, 17
Magee, Bryan, 101
Morris, Tom, xi, xiii, 21, 25, 27
mortality, xi, 1, 3–19, 27

necessities, 71, 74, 75
necessity, 14, 15, 29
    de re, de dicto, 14, 21
nomological, 13, 14, 20, 58

Obitts, Stan, xiv

personhood, 5
Pinnock, Clark, 53
Plato, ix, 4, 52, 72, 78
possibility, 11, 12
    de re, de dicto, 11, 12
properties, immutable, xi, 21, 22, 23
    enduring, 22
    immemorial, 22
    stable, 22
property, 21, 30

Rorty, Richard, x
Rosenbaum, Stephen, 5, 6, 8

Index

self-determination, 16, 17, 46, 61
sinlessness, 25
Smith, Emily Esfahani, 99
Smith, Phil, xiii
Socrates, 30
soul cessation argument, 30, 31
soul cessation, 9, 10, 15, 20, 90
soul euthanasia, 90–102
    types of, 95ff
Spiegel, James, 10, 80–89
structural value, 34ff
suicide, 47, 91, 99–102

Talbott, Tom, 69

Universalism, xii, 90–102

Velveteen Rabbit, 48

Wennberg, Bob, xiii
Williams, Margaret, 48

Yourgrau, Palle, 6

www.ingramcontent.com/pod-product-compliance
Lightning Source LLC
Chambersburg PA
CBHW032234080426
42735CB00008B/849